REVIVAL
EVENT OR LIFESTYLE

STEVE & SALLY
WILSON

ENDORSEMENTS

I highly recommend Revival: Event or Lifestyle to anyone who is longing for another "Great Awakening." Steve and Sally shift the reader from viewing revival through a traditional lens of an extraordinary/occasional event to seeing revival as an everyday lifestyle. This revival impacts every level of church life and society through a practical, personal lifestyle of active faith.

Dr. Tom Jones
Executive Director of Global Awakening
Overseer of the Apostolic Network of Global Awakening (ANGA)

As an avid student of revival, reading Steve and Sally's book on revival as a lifestyle was intriguing and practical. Revival is more than just a church revival meeting held at a particular time of the year. It is not just an event, but more so; it is a way of life for every believer. I long for the day when every individual disciple would understand the way of the Kingdom when it comes to revival and not just wait for an event. Revival is a lifestyle. This book opens an insight to every disciple of Jesus Christ who wants to be a part of what God is doing today. All I can say is, read the book. It will change your thinking and your living.

Dr. Bennett C. Smith, Senior Pastor/Bishop
Legacy Church International
Mobile, AL

Winds of change are blowing. Many feel a new season upon them, but they are unsure of the next step. As a true Father and Mother in the faith, Steve and Sally Wilson have lived the pages in this book. Through their Kingdom lifestyle of love and writing, they have presented us with an extraordinary gift and a navigational roadmap into a supernatural lifestyle.

A captivating read, **Revival: Event or Lifestyle**, *will teach, train, and activate a deeper revival culture in your life, church, and marketplace. Be prepared to behold the present-day glorious Kingdom of our Lord Jesus.*

Mike and Andrea Brewer
Founding Directors of Reach Haiti and Reach International Ministries
Authors of "Pioneering Faith"

It has been a great privilege getting to know Steve and Sally personally. They are an amazing couple that truly lives out a revival lifestyle and their passion has impacted many people, across the globe. Their book **Revival: Event or Lifestyle**, *captures what their whole life is about, living a naturally supernatural lifestyle that passionately pursues the presence of God.*

Within these pages you will be encouraged, inspired and also equipped to be a revivalist, in your everyday life. Steve and Sally's message is one that will empower and release you in your God-given authority to influence the world around you. So let's join together with Steve and Sally and be passionate people of His presence; people who impact their world; people who have encountered the power of the Holy Spirit and people who give it away to others.

Steve and Sonya Little
Senior Pastors
C3 Church Warragul, Australia

REVIVAL

EVENT OR LIFESTYLE

Equipping the Body for a Life of Supernatural Ministry

by

STEVE & SALLY
WILSON

global awakening
lighting fires • building bridges • casting vision

Revival: Event or Lifestyle; Equipping the Body for a Life of Supernatural Ministry by Steve and Sally Wilson

Apostolic Network of Global Awakening
1451 Clark Street
Mechanicsburg, PA 17055

For more information on how to order this book or any of the other materials that Global Awakening offers, please contact the Global Awakening Bookstore.

ISBN: 978-1-944238-01-8

| TABLE OF CONTENTS |

DEDICATION

To the Dayspring Church who have stood with us over the years as we have sought to understand and build a revival culture. Your faith and commitment to Jesus have allowed us to become a revival hub, not known for revival meetings but as a group of people seeking to live a revival lifestyle. Let's continue until the revival presence we have experienced turns into a full-blown awakening in our city, state and nation.

ACKNOWLEDGEMENTS

Special Thanks To

Farley Lewis for proof reading, editing, and valuable suggestions. You have been very helpful in seeing the completion of this book. Thank you for your dedication and tireless effort. You are truly a blessing to Sally and me.

Special Thanks To

Melissa Vanderlinden for your cover design. You have taken our thoughts and captured them into images again. Thank you for sharing your gift with us.

FOREWORD

A year and a half ago I was picked up from the airport and driven to a church that was hosting us for a Power and Love School. The director had called me and said, "This is going to be an easy one; this place is full of expectancy." When I walked through the back door I could feel it thick in the air. I had been a part of the Power and Love lineup for 2 years and excitement was always in the air at them; but this was different. Our team did one of these a month for 10 months of the year. This place was exceptional.

As I walked first to the sound booth to speak with our tech director and make sure he had my stuff for the next morning. He turned and looked at me and said, "You feel that?" I said, 'Most Definitely!" The atmosphere was pregnant with the Presence and the Miraculous. Once I met the Wilsons I understood why. They weren't young, edgy or slick looking leaders. They were people committed to Revival and Awakening. Their humility, yet unbridled Passion for an outbreak of God in their community, was stirring to say the least. I knew I was meeting not just the hosts of our school but Leaders who knew how to host the Presence of God. It wasn't an experience of long ago that they reflected on but a current that ran through them. That week at Dayspring in Springfield, MO, brought fresh understanding to being under an Open Heaven.

When Steve and Sally Wilson talk about **Revival: Event or Lifestyle**, it isn't a light subject they walk you through. You can practically see the calluses on their hands where they have held the dowels that went through the golden rings that carried the Ark. As you read through these pages, starting with Kingdom Culture, they aren't speaking from the bleachers but as those who have lived it. Their coaching on being Anointed as Priests is crucial to seeing any church or movement launch in the atmosphere of the supernatural. The chapter on Power and Authority opens your eyes to understand the invitation of Jesus and the Holy Spirit to actively use what they have deposited in us.

Steve and Sally Wilson aren't just pursuing Revival for themselves and their area, but as you read on, you can tell they are contending for you to have Revival. Brace for Impact! You are about to go on the ride of your life!

Robby Dawkins
International Evangelist and Equipper of Churches.
Author of "Do what Jesus Did" and "Identity Thief"
Featured in several Power Evangelism Documentaries

INTRODUCTION

A couple of years ago we came out of an amazing revival meeting in Brazil. We had just experienced a glorious presence of God where we saw the lame walk, the deaf hear and the blind see. Then at the call to salvation many made their way to the altar in response to the goodness of God they had witnessed. After the meeting, we were standing at the door with one of the pastors when we noticed that across the street stood a group of prostitutes. One of the team pointed it out to the pastor and commented on the contrast to what we had just experienced. I will never forget his answer. He said longingly, "We have revival but we need an awakening!"

A spiritual awakening changes the face of society. There have been many revivals throughout history but few awakenings. An awakening is characterized by its transforming influence outside the church on the surrounding community. When the revival a church experiences becomes a lifestyle for the believers, the awakened church breaks out of its walls and demonstrates the resurrection power of Jesus Christ. The effect of this testimony changes lives, as it challenges ungodly structures and establishes God's righteousness and justice. We should expect that one of the first marks of awakening would be a church motivated to live a revival lifestyle every moment of their lives.

BEND THE CHURCH

Before the Welsh Revival, one of the great spiritual awakenings in history, Evan Roberts heard a phrase that changed his life. He heard a preacher pray, "Bend the Church and save the world." The Holy Spirit used this to bend Roberts to believe for souls and, in the subsequent revival, more than 100,000 souls were swept into the kingdom. We stand today at a defining moment in history; God calls His church to awaken for the field is ready for harvest, yet few appear motivated to move out of their comfort zone and engage with Him in the work of harvest. The Holy Spirit is calling the church to bend away from their earthbound introspection to a kingdom-minded expectancy, to turn their eyes away from the enemy and on to the harvest being orchestrated by their glorious King.

Somehow the church has forgotten her destiny and allowed her attention to be captured by the encroaching evil, rather than the irresistible advance and expansion of the kingdom. The effect of this obsession with the evil around them has caused believers to live with a fortress mentality, confining their faith to the inside of a building. Jesus told us that the wheat and the tares grow together until the harvest. If we understand this correctly, we can expect evil to increase as we move forward in history. But at the same time that the tares of evil mature, the wheat is ripening for the harvest.

Choosing where to focus our gaze will prove a defining trait of those who overcome. Jesus tells us that we cannot let worry control us as we serve Him. We cannot love and serve God and at the same time love and serve mammon. We must choose one or the other. On the surface this looks like a reference to money, but a look at the root word sheds light on our priorities. The word *mammon* comes from Aramaic and carries a meaning of, "that which gives security to self."

So our response to troubling times is to either worry about our own security, or we can enlist in the greatest quest in history. The call on our lives requires us to love God unconditionally and throw ourselves into fulfilling His purpose on the earth in this hour. For those who will take the risk and unconditionally give their lives, there is a stunning promise. Where sin abounds grace abounds more. There is a grace personally and corporately available in this season for those who will press into awakening.

Far from evoking fear, this moment of cultural upheaval should fill us with great anticipation. The Church of Jesus Christ is not losing ground but rather stepping into greater glory as we enter that season of epic conflict between darkness and light. We have the opportunity to respond with unconditional love when confronted by hate for our precious Lord Jesus. The love we demonstrate will produce the greatest outpouring of His glory any of us has ever experienced.

A few years ago when I would still my heart I would hear the phrase, "The level is rising." I began to declare it whenever I heard it and although there was not much in the natural realm to confirm it, I knew I was speaking what heaven was saying. At first, we did not see much change, but slowly we felt the atmosphere shift as more and more of the body embraced the desire to do the works that Jesus did out in society.

All over the world we see the level rising today. We believe this is the first wave of a great awakening that will sweep across the globe. The Spirit of God is calling the church to stir herself to engage with Him in a great end time harvest. Paul tells us that, *it is already the hour for you to awaken from sleep; for now salvation is nearer to us than when we believed* (Rom 13:11). O how we need this exhortation to wake up, to stand up, and to be active in this hour.

FROM REVIVAL TO AWAKENING

In our first book, *Keep the Fire Burning*; we laid out some of the core beliefs and values we found necessary to help us sustain a revival culture within the local church. We learned that the spiritual beliefs and values we held created the environment in our gatherings that in turn governed our activity. We found that as we changed some of our belief structures and adjusted our values to line up with the presence and power of the Holy Spirit we created an atmosphere conducive to sustained revival.

The goal of a revival culture goes beyond wonderful meetings. The purpose of revival is to equip the people of God to carry the presence of God they experience in such a way that they live a world-changing lifestyle. In *Revival: Event or Lifestyle*, we detail some of the beliefs and values that will equip the body to take revival to the streets, allowing the revival we experience in the house to become a true awakening. We want to help bend the church from her introverted self-focus to a lifestyle that affects society outside the church buildings.

The following chapters will provide tools to move the church out of the building and into the marketplace so that the world around them is reached. If an awakening affects the culture, then we need to understand the influence we are to have in the cultures we encounter. We begin by looking at the process of moving churches out of their religious culture and into a true kingdom culture. Such a culture will sustain revival presence until it becomes a lifestyle that in turn ushers in a culture-transforming awakening.

CHAPTER 1

KINGDOM CULTURE

CREATING A CULTURE THAT SUSTAINS A MOVE OF GOD

Tom Jones was to speak on the last night of the "Awakened to Destiny" conference at Dayspring Church in Springfield, MO. When he came up to transition the service, we witnessed a sovereign move of God as the Holy Spirit was poured out. It was glorious! Jessica, one of our youth leaders, released a powerful word about the presence of Jesus in the room. As soon as she finished, she ran down the steps and fell to her knees in front of the platform. Many of the youth rushed over and knelt beside her and, simultaneously, across the congregation a shout broke out. Like a match thrown into gasoline, people started running to the front, some falling, some shaking, some weeping, some laughing and others ministering.

Tom watched as the Spirit of God moved across the congregation. At some point, Steve Swanson, who was leading the worship, noticed that a glory cloud had begun to fill the room and recorded a short video clip on his phone. We do have a hazer that we sometimes use during worship, but we confirmed that it was not working on that night. In fact, when I asked the media team to confirm that it was not operational, they discovered that the binary switches that control it had been manually moved so there was no possibility that what we witnessed was other than the glory of God.

That night Tom preached a little in the glorious chaos of Word and Spirit but the Holy Spirit took charge. The manifest presence of God that night created a defining moment for us as a church. Lives were changed, bodies were healed and the presence of God drew people to the meeting who had no idea what had transpired. One young man who had been running from God lay on his bed a mile away when the same presence we were experiencing fell in his room. He got up, got dressed and came to the building drawn by the presence of God.

When people asked me the following week, "Are we in revival?" I answered, "Yes, but now we must steward what we have been given." Historically, churches start a series of meetings and run them until the presence lifts or until the staff runs out of energy. This comes from a church culture that views revival as primarily a series of events.

Living in revival has to be more than attending nightly meetings, no matter how good they are. Revival should be a lifestyle held in place by a combination of both sovereign action and personal responsibility. We know we will have many blowout meetings and we may well have a regular series of meetings. But God's heart burns for the world. He calls us to live out before them the revival fires we have experienced.

For most churches this requires a change in culture. Traditional church cultures have more to do with preserving the past rather than influencing the society around them. This gives them a predominately inward focus that is counter to a revival culture. This paradigm keeps the revival in the house so that it never grows to become an awakening. The challenge for the church today is to first move from a religious culture to revival culture where hosting the presence of God becomes the priority. Then churches must shift into an outward focused kingdom culture that has the capacity to sustain revival until it becomes an awakening.

WHAT IS CULTURE?

Culture can be defined in many ways but the definition we like defines culture as "an integrated system of learned behavior patterns which characterize the members of a society and which are not a result of biological inheritance."[1]

These behavior patterns are then supported by sets of beliefs and values, which in turn govern their actions. Since culture is learned behavior, we do most of what we do without thinking. It feels natural to us because it is just the way we do it. Little thought is given to the beliefs and values that support culture because they are such an integral part of our life.

Most of us are not even aware of our culture until we find ourselves confronted by people who think or behave differently. The more contact we have with another culture the more aware we become of their patterns of behavior. Understanding culture as learned behavior provides a key to cultural transformation. It means that we can learn to live in and adapt to a new cultural environment.

When we left Africa and moved to England, our children went into the English school system. Because Kenya had been a British colony, the culture was not completely foreign to them, but being an American living in England in the early 80s was not fun. After several years in school, the college in West Yorkshire, which our daughter attended, held a competition to discover who had the most proper British accent. When the competition ended, Rachel had won. Her defense mechanism had so adapted her language and pronunciation that she had cultivated the best BBC accent in the college. You can imagine the considerable consternation on the part of the faculty when they discovered that an American had been given the distinction.

The next conclusion we can draw from our definition indicates that culture is held in place by beliefs and values. If this is true, then when we learn the beliefs and values of a culture, we can relate to the people of that culture. And furthermore, because actions stem from learned behavior, as we learn the beliefs and values we will begin to act like we belong in the new culture. This is critical: If we want to live in a kingdom culture, we must teach and practice new beliefs and values.

KINGDOM CULTURE

One of the earliest memories for many of us is praying the Lord's Prayer. *Your kingdom come, Your will be done on earth as it is in heaven* (Matt 6:10). Little did we understand that we were inviting the rule of God to invade this realm and were calling for the culture of heaven to be established here on earth. At its most basic, kingdom culture is made up of the beliefs and values consistent with the life of heaven being lived out here on earth. The culture we pursue is a culture where each member of the church commits to seeing the will of God done on earth with the same expediency that it is done in heaven.

Therefore, kingdom culture is *learned behavior* held in place and sustained by kingdom-minded beliefs and values consistent with the life and ministry of Jesus and His prayer model - On earth as it is in heaven. This new culture must have as its core value a hunger to create an atmosphere that invites and sustains the presence of God and the free operation of the gifts of the Holy Spirit.

The religious systems that have shaped the church's culture today must be challenged because these systems tend to restrict the flow of the Spirit in favor of tradition. The beliefs and values inherent in these religious systems were formed to preserve the old wineskins rather than to make room for the new wine. The Holy Spirit seeks to put in us a value system that moves us into our destiny as believers and frees us from the bondage of legalism. Churches who allow the Holy Spirit the freedom to shift them into a kingdom culture are the ones that will have a transforming impact on society around them.

SUBCULTURE OR COUNTERCULTURE

I grew up in a conservative, fundamentalist family that held the Word of God in high honor but knew very little about the work of the Holy Spirit. Even on the mission field we were a subculture with little interaction with the world around us. With rare exception, the church for the last few centuries has tended to live primarily as a subculture of society – a church closeted in a building has little effect on the world around them. Webster defines a subculture as a group that has beliefs and behaviors that are different from the main groups within a culture or society. In a subculture, the beliefs and values of the culture isolate it from the rest of society.

When the Supreme Court gave their opinion on Roe v. Wade in 1970, the church disagreed with the decision but largely ignored it. Society did not try to force Christians to go against their conscience and have an abortion. The law did not directly affect the church because they could choose to reject it without consequence. Unfortunately, when the church operates as a subculture it remains an oddity with very little impact on the society.

A counterculture, on the other hand, challenges both the secular and religious norms of society. Webster defines a counterculture as a culture with values and customs that are very different from and usually opposed to those accepted by most of society. When we live as a counterculture the good news gets out of the house and impacts the culture around us. This is either because the dominant culture begins to threaten the churches existence or because the message motivates the church to move outside the walls and share their faith.

Kingdom culture should be a counterculture. The early church did not stay in the upper room. The boldness they displayed as they witnessed for Jesus as the Messiah brought them into direct conflict with the religious leaders of the day. Yet in the midst of their greatest persecution they prayed for even more boldness. *And now, Lord, take note of their threats, and grant that Your bond-servants may speak Your word with all confidence, while You extend Your hand to heal...* (Acts 4:29-30). God answered immediately with another infusion of the Holy Spirit, validating the prayer and the position they had taken. It would appear that boldness and an increase in the miraculous are the two things that must accompany the church if she is to live as a counterculture in society.

Almost immediately, it would seem that the church faced a temptation to stay in Jerusalem where they had already made an impact. Perhaps it had become comfortable and even safe to be a Christian. But the onset of persecution dispersed them with the result that the gospel spread rapidly, introducing a kingdom culture into nation after nation.

For the church in our culture, the recent decisions of the Supreme Court will have an unavoidable and long-term effect. The Obergefell v. Hodges decision redefining marriage has an enormous, direct and immediate impact on the way we live our lives. No longer can the church take a position of avoidance; we will come into direct conflict as society seeks to force us to accept what

God has declared as unacceptable. Christian schools and businesses will continue to be placed in untenable positions where allegiance to God and His Word sets us against cultural norms. While we do not relish the coming conflict, the forced move to live as a counterculture will prove to be one of the best things that has happened to the church in the United States.

CHANGING CULTURE

If we find our churches unprepared for this challenge, something needs to change. Our objective is to understand the process of shifting our churches into a kingdom culture that can sustain revival. In general, culture changes within the church in one of two ways - renewal and reformation. Renewal is where internal changes are made that breathe new life into a church structure. On the other hand, reformation involves a complete overhaul of the beliefs and values to bring them in line with heaven's culture.

Anthropologists use the term "cultural invention" to describe change or innovation that takes place in a culture either through an internal discovery of something useful to the society or from outside pressure forcing change. If you have ever watched the movie "The Gods Must Be Crazy," it is all about cultural invention. A pilot throws a coke bottle out of his window and it lands in a village. The movie is first about the multiple uses the villagers find for this wonderful object that the gods have chosen to give them, followed by the disruption that the change causes. The last half of the movie follows the process of getting rid of the object so they can get things back to normal.

Many churches have found the Holy Spirit and have become charismatic versions of their structure but have not made the changes necessary to fully reflect a kingdom culture. Typically, church cultures have been established to preserve the past instead of unlocking the future; so, for these institutions, it will take more than the addition of some new methods. At some point, they will each need to examine their beliefs and values in light of the life and ministry of Jesus if they hope to make the jump to kingdom culture.

Another term anthropologists use for cultural change is acculturation. The word essentially means the replacement of the traits of one culture with the traits of another. In our context we will use this word to describe the way that heaven's culture impacts and imposes its value system on the church so that the church in turn can impact the world. As difficult as it is, change must come to the church in this season. We must become so desperate to be the church God desires that we will face the pain of change. As one author states, *"Unless we are prepared to give up something valuable, you will never be able to truly change at all, because you'll be forever in the control of things you can't give up."*[2]

TRANSFORMED BY THE SPIRIT

The direct connection between the culture of the kingdom and the work of the Holy Spirit was clearly established by Jesus. He says of Himself, *If I by the Spirit of God cast out demons then the Kingdom of God has come among you* (Matt 12:28 ASV). Jesus demonstrated that whenever the Holy Spirit flowed through Him, it was an expression of the Kingdom of God invading this realm. Thus to live in a Kingdom Culture, we must come to know the presence and power of the Spirit working in and through our lives. Living life empowered by the Spirit serves as the core value that will enable the church to live as a counterculture in society.

This means in practice that every time we allow the Holy Spirit to flow through us, whether through prophecy, word of knowledge, healing or deliverance, the kingdom is advancing. Heaven invades earth and we demonstrate the kingdom's culture here, in this time and place. The anointing of the Holy Spirit is paramount in the declaration and expansion of the kingdom. For the church in this day to have the impact on society that God desires, she must be full of the power and presence of the Holy Spirit. Only then will we operate as a true counterculture that has a real impact on society.

Kingdom culture, which is the culture of heaven touching the earth, advances and expands by the work of the Holy Spirit in and through the life of the believer. So, for us to live as culture-changers, we must live so full of the Spirit that we manifest His presence in every arena of our life. One man or woman fully yielded to the Holy Spirit proves far more dangerous to the enemy in this world than a whole room full of Sunday Christians. For those who would live out a kingdom culture, get acquainted with the Holy Spirit and learn to live and walk in communion with Him.

RULES OR RELATIONSHIP

When we define kingdom culture as a set of beliefs and values that govern our actions, it is easy for us to think *rules* rather than *relationship*. But when we refer to a kingdom culture we are referring to a set of spiritual beliefs or values that create an atmosphere conducive to hosting the presence and power of the Holy Spirit. Paul expands the definition of kingdom culture when he writes to the Romans. He tells the church that, *… the kingdom of God is not eating and drinking, but righteousness and peace and joy in the Holy Spirit* (Rom 14:17).

His definition begins by challenging legalism. Kingdom culture is not made up of a set of rules that determines the way we live. It is not a set of don'ts that keep us from sin. It is not what we eat or do not eat. In fact, it has nothing in common with a list of "do's" and "dont's". For centuries this misconception has kept the church bound up with a legalism that has robbed it, keeping it from expressing a true kingdom culture. Instead of being subject to the Spirit of life, many believers still live in bondage to the law and miss the glorious freedom that comes from a life surrendered to the Spirit.

This does not mean that kingdom culture allows a free-for-all. We have been freed from the law so that we can live by the law of the Spirit. The lordship of the Holy Spirit will ensure that we use our freedom from the law as an opportunity to show love for our brothers and sisters, rather than running the risk of offending them with our freedom. The measure of kingdom culture is not the rules we keep but a life grounded in His righteousness, our message of peace, and our disposition of joy.

ROADBLOCKS

Cultural change in the church has always proved difficult, but there are a few major roadblocks that are relatively easy to identify. One such barrier is past success. When a church has experienced a move of God, they can come to believe their best days are in the past and as such find it difficult to move forward. The more we get to know the Holy Spirit the more we come to realize that He is infinitely creative. Almost every move of God in history has some element that resulted in tripping people up who were not deliberately sensitized to the movement of the Spirit of God. This roadblock of past success tripped up Moses. The first time they needed water, striking the rock was the obedience. But the second time, repeating what he knew worked turned into sin. The obedience for the new move was to speak to the rock.

Tradition is another obstacle, where "the way we have always done it" stands in the way of change. Another is disunity among the leadership or the members. A church divided on their mission and values will be unable to change. There is also the roadblock of control when a church is under the influence of a few people with money and influence. The members of the body are then at the mercy of decisions that have little to do with obedience to the Holy Spirit. A final barrier that is easy to spot is anxiety. When the leadership of a church is insecure, the fear of man produces a disabling fear of change.

Leadership must find ways over, around or through these roadblocks before they can achieve the needed cultural change to bring the church into sustained revival. The rest of this book looks at specific beliefs and values that allow the church to move from a subculture that protects itself from the world to a counterculture empowered to change it.

CHAPTER 2

REVIVAL LIFESTYLE

SPREADING THE FIRE OF REVIVAL INTO THE MARKETPLACE

The final meeting of our November 2014 trip to Beirut, Lebanon, two Lebanese churches and a Pilipino church came together for the service. Then a friend added a whole busload of Syrian refugees to the mix, most from another religious background. (It was an amazing experience to look out over the audience and see such a diverse group.) After the Arabic worship that touched heaven, we gave some words of knowledge and many responded and received their healing.

Then I spoke briefly on the goodness of God and shared a simple salvation message. When I gave the invitation, many responded to the gospel, including most of the Syrian refugees. What a privilege to pour into people hungry for the presence and power of God! The following morning, Nate, one of our team, visited one of the refugee families who had attended the service and asked them what they thought of the meeting. The wife gave a stunning answer. She said, "When I went to the meeting I felt like I was in heaven." God is bringing heaven to earth as He manifests His powerful presence and His love.

A few weeks later, Gaby, pastor of the local church where we met, visited the camps and heard a wonderful testimony from one of the Syrian women who had responded in the meeting. She told him that two days after the meeting, a friend came and told her that she had a tumor; it was on her side and clearly visible. She needed medical help. This new believer, only hours old in the Lord, remembered a testimony I had shared on Sunday. I had told the story of a woman who began to pray for the sick because she saw what Jesus had done in the Gospels and assumed that it must be what Christians do.

This brand new Christian decided that God could use her the same way, so she laid her hands on her friend. The moment she prayed the tumor disappeared! Her friend then asked her to pray for her son. She went to the woman's home and laid hands on the son who had mental problems and he was made whole! It does not stop there. She also prayed for a child who had problems with chronic bedwetting and he was healed.

This is a perfect picture of the move of God in our day. The body is being activated to do the works of Jesus. God looks for our willingness to take the risk and step out. When we do, He stands ready and willing to attest His word with signs and wonders. What we receive in a revival service must affect the way we live our lives. The events that we call revival are designed by God to equip the body for a lifestyle of supernatural ministry.

COMING TO LIFE AGAIN

So what do we hope for when we speak of revival? Church history gives us numerous examples of revivals. We find it easy to pick our favorite and then pray with an expectation that God will do it again. While we should study what He has done in the past, we must take care that we don't miss what God wants to do by putting Him in a box of historical expectations. One thing we have seen is that each revival includes distinct elements with different emphases. Even though we can find commonalities, it has often been the unusual or distinctive component of the move that caused the most conflict.

Many revival accounts give us details of the meetings but little information on the effect the revival had on people, both in and outside of the church. As a result, revival has become associated with meetings so much so that "a series of meetings" is one of the main definitions Webster gives for the word revival. He goes on to define revival as "a period in which something becomes popular again after a long period of time… the growth of something or an increase in the activity of something after a long period of no growth or activity."

While this definition begins to tell the story, there is another facet found only in the origin of the word. The original meaning of the word *revival* when first used in the early 15th century was a "return to consciousness, or to restore to health." So revival carried meanings like, waking out of passivity, regaining consciousness or returning to health. The compound word links the prefix *re-* meaning "again," with the word *vivere*, meaning, "to live."[1] So at its very basic, revival is about coming to life again. We each need to come alive so that we carry the life of God everywhere we go.

TIMES OF REFRESHING

Luke records the verse most often associated with revival. *Therefore repent and return, so that your sins may be wiped away, in order that times of refreshing may come from the presence of the Lord* (Acts 3:19). When His presence is here, so is His refreshing. The context here is repentance and returning. We spend a lot of time teaching on repentance and understand it as a change of direction, but what does the new direction look like? The second word gives the clue.

We are not just to repent; we are to return. The Greek word return used here means "to turn from" and "turn to." When we find this word paired with the word repentance, *metanoeo*, it takes on the idea that believers should repent and return to the fact that sin is forgiven.[2] The righteousness we receive as a gift the moment we repent changes our identity. We move from viewing ourselves as sinners to viewing ourselves as saints, sons and daughters with a restored relationship with our Father. Once sin is forgiven, we need a change of mind in order to walk in the freedom that Jesus purchased for us.

SUSTAINING REVIVAL

Sustaining revival as a lifestyle comes with personal responsibility. Gypsy Smith was a powerful British evangelist. He preached to millions in England

and the US, crossing the Atlantic Ocean over forty times. Everywhere he went revival followed him. One day while speaking to a group of hungry revival seekers, Gypsy revealed his secret. When asked how to carry revival in their lives the way he had, his answer was both simple and profound.

> "Go home. Lock yourself in your room. Kneel down in the middle of the floor, and with a piece of chalk, draw a circle around yourself. There, on your knees, pray fervently and brokenly that God would start a revival within that chalk circle."[3]

The heart of this statement is that sustaining revival is an individual responsibility. True revival awakens us to the power and presence of God with a responsibility to carry that presence out into society and affect others. We are revived so that we will become a people of His presence. We are revived to live out a naturally supernatural lifestyle. We are revived so that everyone we touch will encounter the power and presence of the Holy Spirit. This means that, besides stewarding the fire in our own hearts, the greatest responsibility of a revived people is to give it away to others.

When we begin to carry revival as individuals, the nature of our gatherings will be affected. In a corporate setting, all the individual fires merge to create a furnace that sets other hearts aflame. But the furnace will only sustain as long as individuals maintain their personal walk and responsibility. This is the heart of a revival culture. We love great meetings, but we want to teach the beliefs and values needed to sustain revival through the years. This way we stay alive and don't need constant reviving.

Moody expressed it this way: "The world has yet to see what God will do with and for and through and in and by the man who is fully and wholly consecrated to Him. I will try my utmost to be that man."[4] We believe this is true for every man, woman and child in the body of Christ. The potential in each of us to live our lives full of the power and presence of the Holy Spirit exceeds anything we have yet experienced or even imagined. Let us ask God to give us a hunger for more!

PENTECOST

At Pentecost the church experienced quite a service, but history changed that day because they did not remain in the Upper Room. The presence of

God they experienced caused them to spill into the streets carrying a new lifestyle of power. Thousands were touched by the demonstration of power and were drawn to the truth of the Gospel. The event had so impacted them that even the shadow of Peter as he walked in public proved sufficient to release the powerful presence of God he carried.

The dictionary describes an event as a phenomenon, an observable or extraordinary occurrence. It can also mean a gathering, a ceremony, a meeting or even a party. Our word *event* comes from a Latin word meaning, "to come out, to happen, or to result." This indicates that an event should have a result, a purpose higher than just having a good event. The purpose of an event is to come out into a lifestyle. The purpose of a supernatural event such as a revival meeting is for the people of God to come out into a supernatural lifestyle of revival.

A wedding is an event, the result of a courtship. Courtship led to the wedding event, but the pursuit of courtship needs to continue into marriage as a lifestyle. If the sweet notes and flowers stop on the wedding day – that is, if the event does not lead to a lifestyle – the relationship will never fully develop. Many Christians say, "I do" every Sunday but never develop their relationship with Jesus. They never learn what it means to be partnered with Him in a loving and fruitful relationship. Let's move on into a lifestyle! Remember the event but get on with behaviors consistent with marriage.

EVENT VS. LIFESTYLE

A few years after Pentecost, Jerusalem had been impacted profoundly, but it seems the gospel had not yet touched the region. The persecution that followed the stoning of Stephen led to a mass exodus from the city, but they did not go quietly. Luke tells us that *… those who had been scattered went about preaching the word* (Acts 8:4). Among those scattered was Philip who spread the Gospel into Samaria. The encounter with the Holy Spirit he had in Jerusalem formed in him a lifestyle that birthed a revival.

Let's think for a moment at the contrast between an event and a lifestyle. An event opens the door to the lifestyle; an event has a conclusion, a lifestyle begins new every morning. An event has defined time limits while a lifestyle is timeless with unlimited potential for growth. Events define the present while a lifestyle describes the future. This means that while an event lives in the moment, a lifestyle lives from the moment. An event has a finite purpose while a lifestyle has an infinite purpose. Therefore, we would say that an event is fundamentally unfulfilling unless it leads to lifestyle.

The event of being born again ushers us into a supernatural kingdom where we are called to live. We come out of the event as new creations. The spiritual realm should now become just as real to us as the natural realm. Our spirit comes to life, and we find ourselves capable of receiving instructions from our heavenly Father. The Spirit of God teaches us to hear His voice; then through fellowship, prayer, and the Word we learn and do His will. The new birth connects us to the Spirit and His realm, giving us access to the supernatural wisdom, love and power of Jesus. This initiates a supernatural lifestyle that makes even greater works possible for those who choose to walk in their new identity.

A KINGDOM LIFESTYLE

A kingdom lifestyle is just another way of describing a supernatural lifestyle, a lifestyle punctuated with divine encounters. Jesus connects the works of the Holy Spirit in us to the expansion of the Kingdom of God. He said, *"But if I cast out demons by the Spirit of God, then the kingdom of God has come upon you"* (Matt 12:28). Every time we let the Spirit of God flow through us, we release the Kingdom of God into the world around us. The Holy Spirit serves as the agent of kingdom advancement.

The apostle Paul describes our lifestyle in the Kingdom of God and gives us the building blocks for living a naturally supernatural lifestyle. Paul defines kingdom culture with three words, *For the kingdom of God is not eating and drinking, but righteousness and peace and joy in the Holy Spirit* (Rom 14:17). The context here is culture, eating and drinking, and a discussion on the values we should live by. Into this Paul points to three - righteousness, peace and joy - as the value system of the kingdom revealed to us and held in place by the Holy Spirit. The Holy Spirit works as the agent of change, refining our beliefs and values to fit heaven's value system.

SUPERNATURAL RIGHTEOUSNESS

Heaven's culture requires a revelation of the source of our righteousness because it opens the door to our new identity. The moment we receive Jesus as Savior, we receive Christ's righteousness as a gift, and through it, we inherit the ability to reign in life. *For if by the transgression of the one, death reigned through the one, much more those who receive the abundance of grace and of the gift of righteousness will reign in life through the One, Jesus Christ* (Rom 5:17). The question for believers who wish to carry the awakening today is, "Are you righteous?"

If we depend on our ability to produce righteousness, we will always fall short! But if we put our trust in His grace and the gift of Christ's perfect righteousness, we will step into our destiny. If we do not accept this gift, we live under a cloud of guilt, shame and depression, with no awareness that we have access to His presence. Without His righteousness, we do not feel that our prayers are heard or answered and we cannot convincingly witness because we have no testimony of victory. If we do not understand that we are righteous when we begin to minister, our heart will condemn us and the power of God will not flow freely through us. If we are not righteous, we will not reign in life and a supernatural lifestyle will remain out of reach.

God has accepted and adopted us on the basis of our receiving the perfect righteousness of His Son. This means that as a son or daughter of the King, we have access to the resources of heaven needed to fulfill our destiny. Our commission is the same as we see modeled in the life of Jesus. He came to destroy the works of the evil one. When we embrace the gift of righteousness, we begin to reign through a supernatural lifestyle and participate with Him in destroying the works of darkness.

SUPERNATURAL PEACE

Peace was the good news announced at the birth of Jesus. As the Prince of Peace, He brought heaven's peace to the earth. Peace also describes the nature of the kingdom message the disciples carried as they spread the good news. Kingdom peace is not passivity, far from it. Peace is the atmosphere of heaven released here on earth by the power of the Holy Spirit. From house to house they looked for men and women receptive to the message in whom the peace of the kingdom could be deposited. The power of this peace had the potential to transform culture and usher in His rule.

The emphasis here is on embracing a supernatural lifestyle of peace. Paul prays, *Now may the Lord of peace Himself continually grant you peace in every circumstance* (2 Thess 3:16). Jesus, our Prince of Peace, will grant you peace in every circumstance. He is called our peace in Ephesians 2:14 and in Mark 4:39, He spoke, "Peace! Be still!" to the wind and the sea. Heaven's peace wants to invade earth through us.

His peace in us has the power to change the circumstances around us. *The God of peace will soon crush Satan under your feet...* (Rom 16:20). God's presence manifests in us as peace – each footstep releases peace! His presence manifested through peace is the agency through which the final defeat of the enemy takes place. When we walk in fellowship with the God of peace, the enemy is defeated and under our feet.

SUPERNATURAL JOY

The third manifestation of the kingdom, joy, becomes the disposition of our lives. Webster defines disposition as "the predominant or prevailing tendency of one's spirit; natural, mental, and emotional outlook or mood; to become their characteristic attitude." For people who have experienced the fullness of the Spirit, this makes perfect sense. When we see the victory of the King, despite all the negative circumstances around us, we should be the most joyful people on the earth. In our first book *Keep the Fire Burning,* we shared in depth on how to shift our understanding of joy from an event to a lifestyle.

Supernatural joy should become our lifestyle. The experience of joy should lead us to live from joy. In recent revivals, when joy manifested as laughter, it offended many who did not accept that it was appropriate. What we have come to realize is that joy and laughter are to our great salvation what tears are to repentance. The experience of salvation releases us into a life of joy. *Now may the God of hope fill you with all joy and peace in believing, that you may abound in hope by the power of the Holy Spirit* (Rom 15:13). The Holy Spirit is at work in us to move us into a lifestyle of joy.

The Holy Spirit's role is to reveal Jesus, which means that the fruit of the Spirit are simply character traits of Jesus revealed and worked into our character by the Spirit. Paul lists the fruit as ...*love, joy, peace, patience, kindness, goodness, faithfulness...* (Gal 5:22). For us to live like Jesus, joy must become our regular disposition and not just an occasional experience. Mother Teresa said, "Joy is a net of love by which you can catch souls." Let the joy of our salvation become an identifying mark of our kingdom lifestyle.

DEFINING MOMENTS

Events serve as defining moments that can change our lives forever and move us into a supernatural life. Understood properly, defining moments can free us from our past and connect us to the future. The storms of life produce defining moments because our response to them sets patterns for our life. Defining moments are designed to move us into a new place of action, so that while they shape the future, they do not limit the future. We never forget the moment, but if we focus on the moment, we miss the life lesson.

Do not let our defining moment trap us in history, but make them a spring-board to freedom. Defining moments provide prophetic opportunities, but it is up to us what we do with them. For Peter, walking on water was a defining moment. But his moment was not defined by sinking but by stepping out. As far as we know he did not try it again, the event did not define Peter's future action, but it did define his future focus – keep our eyes on Jesus!

A life with God is full of events that should shape our lifestyle. The event is the building block for our future. The event of repentance is necessary to live in salvation. The event of forgiveness clears the way for us to live in wholeness. Surrender is necessary to live under His Lordship in the same way that the event of baptism in the Spirit is necessary to live a Spirit-filled life.

The goal of each encounter is not the experience but the lifestyle it produces. We needed to be born to have a life, but the experience of birth does not need to be repeated for the life to be real. Too many people are living from event to event and never allow it to become a lifestyle. When the event is over, their experience is over and they slip back into life as usual. Events rightly under-stood and applied properly lead to life transformation, but human nature too often lives in the event and misses the message. On the Mount of transfiguration, the disciples wanted to build a tabernacle to memorialize the event, but Jesus wanted them to taste the supernatural life.

THE AWAKENING

God has called the church to develop and sustain a culture where the supernatural becomes natural, a church where each member of the body seeks to live life in obedience to and under the influence of the Holy Spirit, to be a church where the power of God is welcome so that the world can witness the goodness of God displayed through His people. We believe that through a revival lifestyle, sustained by a revelation of the priesthood of the believer, we will witness the impossible become not just possible, but normal.

C H A P T E R   3

ANOINTED
AS PRIESTS

RELEASING EVERY BELIEVER INTO MINISTRY

I recently did a Sunday morning service at another church. I planned to share about the goodness of God and knew that God wanted to demonstrate His goodness in a tangible way. When I arrived I discovered that the daughter of the pastor had suffered from intense back pain for weeks and had planned to stay home, but her parents persuaded her to come and believe for healing. A group gathered around her at the beginning of the service and prayed but saw no change. During worship, I could see the agony on her face and knew she would not stay much longer without some relief.

I asked the Holy Spirit what to do and He dropped a thought into my head. When I got up to speak, I asked her to stand and then asked the youngest child in the room who could speak to come up and help me. This amazingly bold 4 year old responded and I asked her to lay her hand on the daughter's back and command it to be healed in Jesus' name. After the first prayer, the daughter felt a significant improvement. I encouraged the little girl to pray again, and this time, when the woman checked her back out the pain was gone. God broke through that morning through a child simply willing to step out.

THE BELIEVER'S PRIESTHOOD

Much of what we understand about the priesthood of the believer gets filtered through our religious tradition. Most of the time we are not even aware of it. As we seek to equip the body of Christ to do the work of ministry, our understanding of what each member of the body is called to do and to be is crucial. While writing the notes for teaching this subject, I heard the Holy Spirit say that: "the religious spirit has tainted our understanding of the priesthood of the believer." We can measure our understanding by the response to the story we just told. Some will rejoice that a child can be used, but the religious spirit fears this truth. So let's lay a foundation in our hearts for something that we may already believe, but possibly don't fully understand.

In creation there was no mention of or need for a priesthood. However, we can see a foretaste of the call and responsibility placed on men and women who live in right relationship with God. Adam and Eve enjoyed perfect fellowship with their creator, walking each day in intimacy with Him. From this relationship God commissioned them to rule and subdue as an extension of His rule here on the earth. God's command to rule was Adam and Eve's commission to maintain the culture of heaven so that the earth would become a true reflection of heaven's value system. His command to subdue was their instruction to disallow anything contrary to the nature of the Kingdom of God.

From creation, God's intention is that men and women live in a place of uninterrupted intimacy with Him. From this place of intimacy, we then operate in our priestly function, representing Jesus to a lost and dying world. As priests, each believer has the authority to rule and subdue within their sphere of influence.

THE REFORMATION

In the 1500s, Martin Luther received a revelation of the truth of the gospel and sought to bring reform to the established church. Several of the things he wrote during that period have become cornerstones of our protestant doctrine. Luther had a revelation of faith and penned *Sola Fide,* arguing that justification comes by faith alone. He wrote about grace, *Sola Gratia*, affirming that grace and not works give the foundation for our hope. He taught *Sola*

Scriptura where the word of God alone gives us the authority for our beliefs. These three are still essentials for Protestant believers, including those of us in charismatic churches. We must ensure that everything we believe and practice flows from grace and faith rooted in scripture, rather than as products of tradition.

Another of Luther's writings, *Solas Cristus,* laid the foundation for our understanding of the priesthood of the believer. Luther understood that Christ alone was our high priest. He alone intercedes for us before the Father, meaning that we do not need another priesthood. Although Martin Luther never developed the priesthood of the believer as a theology, what he taught gave the framework for what we understand today.

The religious spirit hates these truths and seeks to pervert them. The religious spirit values form over faith, ensuring that things are done in the proper religious order. Religion values works over grace. The religious system values the work done in the church, rather than the grace that God has released. Religion values tradition over the Word, because it values the way we have done it in the past more than what the Spirit of God is doing in this moment. And finally, religion values clergy over laity.

THE CALL TO MINISTRY

The foundational doctrines of faith, grace and the authority of Scripture have been taught fairly well over the years, but we have not focused enough on the priesthood of the believer. As Protestants, we believe in the priesthood of the believer and teach that through the blood of Jesus we have direct access to God. We no longer need a priest to mediate, because Jesus as our high priest has torn the veil that separated us from the Father. Our access to the Father as priests is a precious truth, but being a priest is more than that, it is also a call to ministry.

Protestants today have been good at removing the idea of priest as mediator. However, we have fallen behind when it comes to the idea that every believer is a minister. Because this has not been fully embraced, we have never completely dismantled the false divide between clergy and laity, nor have we healed the breach between secular and sacred. Consequently, we have not fully released the body to minister; so they wait for leaders to do it. Changing this flawed paradigm requires urgent attention if we are to see the body of Christ carry the awakening to the world. We contend that leaderships' primary role must change to focus on equipping the body to do the work of ministry.

PRIESTS AND LEADERS

From our research, most of the discussion on the priesthood of the believer swings from the "universal priesthood" view to a full dismissal of any leadership whatsoever. In the first, the believer's priesthood is limited to offering praises and intercession. The latter rejects the concept of the church as a gathering of people, viewing every individual believer as a church. Somewhere between these extremes the truth hides.

Some of the confusion seems to originate from the usage of two Greek words; *hiereus*, which means "sacred one" and *presbyteros* meaning "elderly or older." The word *hiereus* is translated in most versions as "priest," while the word *presbyteros* is generally translated as "elder." In the Douay-Rheims Bible the word *presbyteros* was transliterated into Latin as *presbyter* and then shortened to priest when translated into English.

The earliest records from church history show no evidence that there was any organized office using the word *hiereus* other than the recognition of Jesus as our high priest. They do, however, record the role of *presbyteros*, (elder) and *episkopos* (usually meaning overseer). While this word is transliterated bishop, it would appear that it could also be used to refer to the role of any fivefold ministry gifts that give care to the body.

Thus the idea of elders indicates a category of leadership separate from our priesthood as believers. There should not be confusion here; every believer is a priest, a sacred one (*hiereus*, the word used in 1 Pet 2:5); not every believer is an elder (*presbyteros*), though the word was occasionally translated into English as priest.

THE TRANSITION

A fresh pattern of leadership emerged in the early church. Fivefold ministry gifts served to equip believers for the work of ministry, while each church appeared to have elders who provided local wisdom and leadership. Although these leaders did minister, they understood that their primary role was to release the body into ministry. They led with a revelation that the priesthood of the believer was a call for every individual to operate as a minister of God on behalf of the people they encountered. In this environment every individual felt empowered to share his or her faith.

In about A.D. 312, a far-reaching transition took place when Constantine converted to Christianity. His "Edict of Toleration" ended persecution and began a shift that resulted in Christianity becoming the official religion of the Roman Empire. This historic upheaval was not without its challenges. Rather than getting you killed, suddenly being a Christian could get you ahead in business or politics. The cost of following Jesus moved from sacrifice to expedience. Since it was now advantageous to be a Christian, the new low-cost identity meant that churches found themselves flooded with nominal believers. Fathers no longer understood the foundations of faith to train their children or lead their families in spiritual things.

When the fathers could no longer train their kids, a professional was hired to do the job for them. A professional priest took over the spiritual business for the people who could no longer do it for themselves, and the people shifted their focus to the secular. To this day, we suffer the effects of this devastating transition that created the clergy-laity divide. We believe this giant must come down as the Holy Spirit challenges the body of Christ to return to the priesthood of the believer as God had intended.

At Mount Sinai when God met with His people, He called out their destiny. *You shall be to me a kingdom of priests and a holy nation* (Exod 19:6). He views His people a kingdom of priests. This description of their call occurs before the Levitical priesthood was established. So God is expressing His ultimate desire. His intention for His people was that we would become a kingdom of priests, that every single man and woman would operate as a priest before Him. He defines them as a nation of priests. They would all have access to His presence, they would walk in the anointing, and they would do His will.

We find it interesting that God lays out this priestly intention for His people almost immediately after Jethro brought his correction to Moses. Remember, Moses had been doing all the leading and resolving disputes himself, but Jethro pulled him aside and told him what he was doing was not good. In fact, he said exactly what God said about Adam in the garden. The one-man leadership model is not the right mechanism for bringing the people to maturity. Moses responded by delegating his leadership, and into this atmosphere of plurality God says, I'm going to make you "a kingdom of priests."

Regardless of what has happened in church history, God's intention for us is clear: *But you will be called the priests of the Lord; You will be spoken of as ministers of our God* (Isa 61:6). Can you see what the New Covenant looks like? Every believer functions as a priest and every believer can operate as a minister. From the youngest to the oldest, male or female, rich or poor, there is no division of who can minister because we are a kingdom of priests. What a glorious truth - to be identified as ministering priests.

The Hebrew word Isaiah used means "serving as a minister."[1] The word described a function, not an office or position. Catch that, ministry is a functional word, not a positional word. God's intention is that every man, woman and child in His body would function as a ministering priest for Him, by expressing His love to the world around them. If we begin to believe and act on this, it would change the way we live our lives.

Martin Luther once wrote that he wished the word priest would become as common as the word Christian[2] because all Christians are priests. That is powerful. What if the word priest was as common as the word Christian today? What if the idea of ministry felt as normal as the idea of being a Christian? What if literally every believer in every place began to operate in his or her function as priest before God? It would change society because the message of the kingdom of God would get outside the walls.

The C.S. Lewis Institute quotes a teaching that Luther gave that the milkmaid and the plowman could do priestly work.[3] This was totally revolutionary for his day. But he even took it further, contending that the plowing and the milking were priestly works. Can we get that? The fact that we are there in our workplace means it is our place of ministry. We are carriers of the life of God to our workplace. This idea of priest as ministry is consistent with Luther's view that to be a priest means to be a priest for someone. Luther's call was not a call to seclusion. It was a call to serve God and serve others. This understanding of the priesthood of the believer is consistent with our commission to function as a kingdom of priests and as a light to the nations.

If the church would begin to teach this, then in whatever profession we find ourselves, we would serve in our priestly function. We would work in our employment both as a laborer and as a priest. We would do our work as priests of the living God in such a way that we would carry the life of God into that environment. Living this way we lose the secular/sacred nonsense that has messed with the church. We also get away from thinking that our behavior in the workplace is just business. If we are priests at work, then our ethics on the job must match our ethics at a church event. We cannot change ethics for our business practices.

Smith Wigglesworth served as a plumber for most of his life. His occupation did not limit his ministry; it provided an opportunity for ministry. He saw many plumbing customers healed and saved because he did not distinguish between the secular and sacred. He just lived a life of ministry. Reese Howells, one of the great intercessors, worked in a coal mine for much of his life. The coalmine did not affect his intercession because his life was yielded to the Holy Spirit even while he worked. He was not an intercessor on Sunday and a coal miner on Monday. He was a priest wherever he was. Could this change the way we live our lives?

When we see that plumbing or working in a coal mine is just as spiritual as working in the church, then our workplace becomes the arena for the exercise of our faith. If the church will teach that working in business, medicine, politics, in fact any profession provides the context for believers' priestly function, it will release people to impact the world around them. What would the world be like if every believer lived as a priest, releasing both salt and light? What if every believer would operate as a priest doing his or her job for God's glory? If we did, we could permanently destroy the secular vs. sacred lie!

Peter told believers that, *you also, as living stones, are being built up as a spiritual house for a holy priesthood, to offer up spiritual sacrifices acceptable to God through Jesus Christ* (1 Pet 2:5). This verse teaches that the building is not the holy house; rather, it is the believers themselves who make up the dwelling place. If we come to church, then we come to get touched by something. However if we are the church, we carry something with us everywhere we go. Peter tells us here that as believers we carry the responsibility of ministering as priests wherever we go.

Believers are a priesthood who are built together into a spiritual house. As a spiritual dwelling, we house the Holy Spirit both individually and corporately. So every believer is a priest, a walking spiritual house through whom the Holy Spirit can function. As a priest our parish may be the grocery store, or in our own business, or a restaurant, or wherever we happen to go or work. Our sphere of influence as a priest extends into all areas of society. Wherever the spiritual house goes it affects society. This priestly function derives directly from Jesus our high priest who calls each of us to share in his priestly ministry.

As priests we are called to offer spiritual sacrifices. The emphasis here is not on our access to God but on our priestly function of sacrificing on behalf of others. So what is a spiritual sacrifice? When we look through the New Testament at every time the word sacrifice is used in relation to our lifestyle, it will get us closer to the answer. Notice as we go through these that every one can happen in life, not just in meetings. We believe that what happens in the lives of believers between worship services is just as much church as any meeting. As we live in this truth, we will begin to transform our world.

SPIRITUAL SACRIFICES

In Matthew 9:13, spiritual sacrifice is defined as showing compassion. God wants compassion from us rather than a sacrifice based in legalism. If we show compassion to someone at work, we just offered a spiritual sacrifice. If somebody behaves like a bear and we show gentle compassion, we just offered a spiritual sacrifice. By showing compassion we fulfill our priestly responsibilities. If somebody spreads rumors about us and our response to them instead is loving, we just became a priest at work. The more compassion we show, the greater the glory we give to God by offering a pleasing and acceptable sacrifice.

In Romans 12:1, the living sacrifice is the whole of our life. The reasonable response to our salvation calls us to lay down our lives for this gospel. Some may have specific callings that put them in positions where they lead or communicate more than others. Scripture makes plenty of room for that. But the call is for every believer to operate in the destiny we were designed for. Everybody needs willingly to give his or her life as a sacrifice. If we choose to live our lives as a sacrifice, position is irrelevant. It's only geography. It's about abiding in the vine so that we bear fruit, regardless of what we do for a living. If our life centers on being a living sacrifice in every moment of our day, then our life becomes a spiritual sacrifice. We are learning what it means to seek first the kingdom of God.

The spiritual sacrifice mentioned in Ephesians 5:2, is to walk in love. Love becomes a sacrifice when we are patient and kind to people who have done nothing to deserve our love. When people betray us and we still choose to love them, it is a spiritual sacrifice. If we will love unconditionally, we will be living as a priest, because living with unconditional love is the very spiritual sacrifice we are called to give.

In Philippians 2:17, a spiritual sacrifice is described as faith. Every time we take a risk, every time we step out in faith, every time we pray for somebody in public, we offer a spiritual sacrifice. Taking an active risk is a spiritual sacrifice given as part of our priestly role. The spiritual sacrifice for faith exercised in the marketplace has no less value than the spiritual sacrifice made by standing on a platform. There is no distinction. There is no difference because the priesthood of the believer encompasses every arena of life.

In Philippians 4:18, a spiritual sacrifice involves giving our finance. Every time we give with joy, it is an acceptable sacrifice. Every time we pay it forward in a grocery store or give the waitress a bigger tip, we have chosen to operate in our priestly function. This goes to the root of how we see money and the way we spend it. Someone once said, "God can get it to you if He can get it through you."

Hebrews 13:15 lists praise and thanksgiving as spiritual sacrifices. Each time we praise God with a thankful heart, it is a spiritual sacrifice. Each time we express thankfulness even in adversity it becomes a fragrant sacrifice to God. Every time we give a word of testimony, telling what Jesus has done, we operate as the priest that God called us to be. When we worship Him with our lives, we personify the truth of the priesthood of the believer.

Our calling as believers is to offer spiritual sacrifices by continually giving ourselves to others. When we touch people with our compassion, our love, our faith and our testimony, these spiritual sacrifices direct people to the goodness of God. It does not direct them to how wonderful or how special we are, but how incredible He is. It directs them to our amazing God who has chosen to use people who will praise and worship Him, to display His goodness in every aspect of their lives.

DOING GOOD AND SHARING

The writer of Hebrews expands the sacrifice from the intimacy of praise and worship to doing acts of kindness. *And do not neglect doing good and sharing, for with such sacrifices God is pleased* (Heb 13:16). God takes pleasure in sacrifices that require us to interact correctly with others. This is evident by the use of the Greek word *koinonia*, which means sharing, fellowship, community and joint participation. In other words, part of our sacrifice is maintaining correct relationships.

The other word used here to describe our spiritual sacrifice is "doing good." This word carries the meaning of good deeds motivated by love. The closest English word to this is "beneficence" which is "a charitable act or gift or the act of doing good; kindness." This was the way Jesus lived His life and the way we are called to live ours. Thus, the second commandment to love our neighbor is the heart of the gospel.

We have seen that the priesthood of the believer means that every believer has been given both access to God through Jesus' blood and a commission to minister to others. This call to service is costly because it involves a life of sacrifice, laying our lives down for our neighbor.

CHAPTER 4

GENEROUS LOVE

INTERRUPTING THE JOURNEY TO SHOW COMPASSION

In 1953, my parents arrived in Kenya as missionaries. The year before they arrived, the British Government declared a state of emergency due to the Mau Mau uprising. The Mau Mau were guerrilla freedom fighters mostly from the predominant Kikuyu tribe who attacked vehicles and settlements in the country in an attempt to overthrow colonial rule. My father, recently discharged from the military, found himself in charge of the home guard for our mission station, in the heart of Kikuyu country. It proved a difficult time for all of us, as we had come to love these people who now threatened our safety.

Some of my earliest memories include images of the barbwire surrounding the buildings and hearing stories of the violence that threatened to destabilize the nation. Each night I fell asleep to the sound of car horns. Every home on the station had a battery-powered horn mounted in their chimney and at appointed times through the night each home sounded their horn in a pre-appointed sequence to signal that all was well. We felt profound relief when the conflict ended, grateful that my dad never had to fire a shot in our defense. In fact, stories emerged after the emergency about attempts to raid our station that were quelled by Divine intervention.

One of my favorites was of the night a group of Mau Mau apparently came to our station for an attack. We learned years later that when they arrived at the railway underpass leading to our property, they were met by what they described as several shining beings that scared them so badly that they fled back into the forest. Incidentally, the underpass they approached was less than 100 yards from our home, making us the first home they would have raided. Thank God for His angelic protection.

In those days, fear was the normal stuff of life and even after the emergency ended the fear in our household only increased. In October 1952, the year before we arrived in Kenya, as part of the crackdown on the freedom fighters, a man named Jomo Kenyatta was arrested and imprisoned for alleged support of the movement. Years later he was released to a hero's welcome, and in 1963, he took office as president when the nation of Kenya received her independence. Because of my father's role as head of the home guard, he feared he was a prime target for retaliation.

On the night of independence, my parents had suitcases packed in our home, nervously awaiting the first speech from President Kenyatta. As we listened to his speech on the radio we hung on every word, waiting for the accusations we felt sure would come. But they didn't. Instead of retribution, he released reconciliation with every word. It stands out as one of the most healing moments in my life. That night His Excellency Mzee Jomo Kenyatta became one of my heroes. He did the impossible. Not only did he initiate healing to the black and white division, he managed to reach out to the Indian community and even temporarily bridged tribalism. The heart of what he shared that night was that we must be willing to suffer without bitterness.

THE GREATEST COMMANDMENT

One day a Pharisee asked Jesus to identify the greatest commandment. Jesus replied, *And He said to him, "You shall love the Lord your God with all your heart, and with all your soul, and with all your mind. This is the great and foremost commandment. The second is like it, you shall love your neighbor as yourself. On these two commandments depend the whole Law and the Prophets"* (Matt 22:37-40). The greatest commandment has two parts combining the Old Testament injunctions found in Deuteronomy 6:5 and Leviticus 19:18.

First, we must love God with all our heart, soul and mind. It is our highest calling to yearn for Him until our minds fill with the wonder of His goodness and the grace He extends toward us. This serves as the first and greatest commandment because it provides the foundation out of which all other aspects of our relationships flow. If our love for God remains pure, then our responses, affections and love for others will follow.

LOVE OUR NEIGHBOR

The second part, to love our neighbor as ourselves is an extension of the first. This second part flows out of the same nature as the first. It shares an equal importance and validity with the command to love God. The command to "love our neighbor as ourselves" demands that we give it the same attention as we do the first. In fact, the injunction to love our neighbor occurs eight times, making it one of the most repeated in Scripture.

In the Old Testament, the law connected loving our neighbor with not taking vengeance or holding a grudge (Lev 19:18). In the New Testament, Matthew ties this instruction to honoring our parents (Matt 19:19), while Paul tells us that it sums up all the commandments (Rom 13:9). Finally, James calls the command to love our neighbor the royal law and tells us that, if we keep it, we will do well (Jas 2:8).

We can never fully love our neighbor without first loving God and accessing His love. Conversely, we cannot claim to love God and disregard our relationships with others. Thus loving God and loving our neighbor are interconnected instructions. We cannot do one without the other. These two work as interdependent parts of the same truth. This means that on some level we can measure the depth of our relationship with God by the quality of our relationships with those around us. John wrote, *If someone says, "I love God," yet hates his brother, he is a liar. For anyone who does not love his brother, whom he has seen, cannot love God, whom he has not seen* (1 John 4:20).

The sobering implication of this verse is that fulfilling the call of God on our lives on some level depends on how well we manage to maintain love in the relationships around us. Everything God requires of us is encapsulated in these two statements. They work together to provide the framework for the whole of the Christian life. Everything Moses and the prophets spoke of and looked forward to begins with loving God and loving our neighbor. Everything that has been written reflects this motive; to draw people to love God and to have real love for one another. This is the measure of Christian maturity.

RESTORED RELATIONSHIP

The heart of the gospel is a restored relationship with our Creator. Before the fall, Adam and Eve lived in perfect fellowship with God. Every evening they visited with their Creator who communed with them in fellowship and harmony. They did not know sin because they shared a nature with God, a nature pure and unstained by evil. They knew no lack; the garden contained everything they needed and more, available at any time they desired. They also had purpose. The Creator had given them the commission to rule together over their environment. I am sure that in the daily briefings with God they discussed their responsibilities in the course of simple, pure fellowship.

Then one day it changed. The father of lies questioned God's provision, pointing out that the fruit from a very desirable tree was forbidden. In the midst of total provision he sold the lie that God was holding out on them and mankind fell. Sin entered the perfection of Eden and mankind found themselves driven from paradise, waiting for a Savior.

Fellowship with God became distant and dependent on animal sacrifice. The fall replaced the perfect natures God had given men and women in creation, with a sinful nature full of judgments, anger, jealousy, frustration and even murder. The full provision of the garden was replaced by hard, unyielding ground covered with weeds and thorns. And the unique purpose man and woman had shared together gave way to a distorted power struggle.

Then Christ came as the last Adam. He lived a perfect life before the Father; He fulfilled all righteousness and went to the cross to pay the price for our redemption. The blood of the Son made a way for full restoration. All that man lost in the fall, Jesus has made available to those who will receive His gift of redemption. Along with the restored relationship came a new nature given as a gift of grace. The resources of heaven belong once again to us as sons and daughters of the King. And the purpose of God for man distorted in the fall is once again made accessible to those who yield to the Holy Spirit.

Jesus' sacrifice restored the fellowship connection with our Creator that was lost in the fall. We can again come into a relationship with the Father because of the blood of the Son. We find this foreshadowed in the Old Testament. When God instructed Moses to build the tabernacle, He gave attention to the detail of each piece. In the description of the Ark of the Covenant, we find a graphic illustration of the restored agreement we now have. God told Moses to build a cover for the ark called the mercy seat. At the mercy seat once a year the blood of the sacrifice would be sprinkled. But look at what else God told Moses, He said: *"I will meet with you there"* (Exod 25:22). The word *meet* used here is the same word translated *agreement* in Amos 3:3. God promised Moses that over the blood of the sacrifice their agreement would be restored. God and man could again fellowship face to face as a man talks to his friend (Exod 33:11).

The stunning beauty of this promise extends to us; the blood of the Son remains on the mercy seat today, giving us access to the Father and a fully restored relationship for those who will put their trust in the blood of Jesus. Scripture also makes it clear that this restoration has both a vertical and a horizontal component. We have a restored vertical relationship with God and a restored horizontal relationship of fellowship with one another.

WE NEED ONE ANOTHER

Amanda had a tumor growing in her throat, but she had learned to trust the Lord through several health issues. She had received more than her share of bad doctor reports, but God had always brought her through. A year earlier, doctors had found a new mass on her thyroid and each subsequent ultrasound confirmed what she could feel every time she swallowed, the tumor was growing. Amanda had developed a strong faith, which she frequently expressed in her prayer life by telling God, "I'm good."

As the tumor grew, the Holy Spirit began to convict her that each time she told God, "I'm good," she was not just saying, "I trust You, Lord," but that she was also saying, "I did not need the prayers of others." One Sunday morning in October of 2015 during an invitation, she once again said, "I'm good." But this time she heard God answer, "No, you're not good - you need this body. You need My bride! I did not call you to be self-sufficient." So she swallowed her independence and went forward for prayer. When the team prayed for her, she felt a peace, an assurance that she was no longer in the battle alone.

The next evening she attended class at the Dayspring School of Supernatural Ministry, and when the speaker gave the invitation for those who needed prayer, she thought, "Lord, I did that yesterday, I'm good." And again she heard the Spirit speak, "I told you, I have placed healing in the body." He showed her different people in the room, and she heard, "There is healing in him. There is deliverance in her..." She went up again for prayer and this time the Spirit came on her so powerfully that she had to lie down. While she lay there she began to feel heat in her throat, then one of the leaders came over to her and said, "You have something to declare." Amanda declared how the King lowered His scepter for Esther, a sign of his mercy. She spoke, "He was saying no to death - Life is granted!" In that moment Amanda swallowed, and realized that she had no obstruction or pressure in her throat!

The next Friday Amanda was scheduled for a biopsy, but when she went in, the doctor could not find the tumor - only a shadow where it had been. They never did the biopsy - there was nothing to investigate. Since that time Amanda has had no problem with her thyroid.

In a nation that holds independence and self-sufficiency as high values, the idea that we are truly interdependent cuts across our cultural norms. As believers, the body of Christ gives us a context where we can practice loving our neighbor while we develop lasting relationships with one another. But the command to love our neighbor does not stop with those in the body. It must become a way of life. Loving those who God has placed close to us has value, but the command extends beyond our Christian brothers and sisters and out to the people we encounter in the rest of our daily life. The command to love our neighbor, in fact, has no boundaries.

WHO IS OUR NEIGHBOR?

When asked the question "Who is my neighbor" (Luke 10:29), Jesus responded by telling the story of the Samaritan who helped a stranger in need by the roadside. In the parable the priest, the Levite and the Samaritan saw the person in need, but only one stopped to help. The need registered with all three, but when the Samaritan saw the man in distress something happened in his heart. Jesus said that he felt compassion! What he saw caused him to feel compassion and the compassion moved him to action. Unlike sympathy that simply identifies with the pain or emotion of a situation, compassion has a power which starts where sympathy leaves off. True compassion moves us beyond feeling and into action.

Our neighbor, then, is the one we stop and trouble ourselves to help. Our neighbor is the next person in front of us. Anyone to whom we can demonstrate the goodness of God and allow them to experience the love of the Father becomes our neighbor. We respond to them in the same way we would want God to respond to us.

Jesus ends the parable with a commission. Go and do like the Samaritan (Luke 10:37). In essence, Jesus tells us to live with an awareness of the needs around us, a willingness to be touched with compassion for those we see, and then to trouble ourselves to help them. We must decide in advance that we are willing to stop and minister to them in order to give them an opportunity for a divine encounter. *My children, our love should not be just words and talk; it must be true love, which shows itself in action* (1 John 3:18 GNT).

Ryan worked with a woman in an industrial laundry mat. The day had been stressful, and emotions were running high. Both Ryan and the woman were grumpy and defensive. She had a fractured bone in her left hand so that she was barely able to perform her work, a job that required both hands. The hand was swollen and painful, and she wore a brace on it.

In the middle of an argument, Ryan "came to" and told her, "I have not even prayed for you. Give me a hug and let me pray for your hand." As he prayed, her hand grew warm. Shortly afterward, she left for lunch.

When she returned, she was excited, waving her hand at Ryan. She said, "Ryan! Look!" She opened and closed her hand, and showed him that the swelling was completely gone. She had no pain at all in her hand, and she had taken off the brace.

Loving our neighbor deals with our innate selfishness. What Ryan did went against the desires of our human nature and demonstrated unconditional love that can only come from the heart of Jesus. Whether they appreciate us or respond to our love, He calls us to love them, and love is practical. Loving our neighbor provides the arena where the nature of Christ is worked into us. *Let each of you look out not only for his own interests, but also for the interests of others* (Phil 2:4 NKJV).

THE NATURE OF CHRIST

If we want to do what Jesus did, we must behave like Him in the way we live our lives and in the way we do ministry. We read that *Jesus was going through all the cities and villages, teaching in their synagogues and proclaiming the gospel of the kingdom, and healing every kind of disease and every kind of sickness* (Matt 9:35). At first glance, it sounds like a preaching tour, but it turned into much more than that. It included an exercise in personal identification with the needs He encountered. Read the next verse; *Seeing the people, He felt compassion for them, because they were distressed and dispirited like sheep without a shepherd* (Matt 9:36).

When He looked at the people, His perspective went past the crowd to focus on the individual needs he encountered. His heart was moved with feelings that compelled Him to action. We encourage every believer to pray this prayer, "I want to see what You see and I want to feel what You feel." It is a great prayer, but if we pray it, we must make sure we prepare ourselves for the encounter of a lifetime. Just look at a couple of the words Jesus used to describe what He saw. He saw them as *distressed*; the Greek word used here has a variety of meanings "including to be stripped down or mangled." The second word He uses is *dispirited* which also means "to be thrown down, to be thrown out or scattered."[1]

Look through His eyes for a moment. Both words graphically describe the destructive work of the enemy in the lives of the people. They have been subjected to the ravages of the kingdom of darkness and its destructive tyranny. The people He saw are the people He loved. What is His response? He will personally go to the cross for their redemption. But in the next verse He commissions His disciples, and by extension us, to serve as His hands and feet in the harvest. He calls us to partner with Him in bringing the deliverance they so desperately need. *Then He said to His disciples, "The harvest is plentiful, but the workers are few. Therefore beseech the Lord of the harvest to send out workers into His harvest"* (Matt 9:37).

LOVE HAS HANDS

The harvest goes beyond street witnessing or evangelistic crusades. There is nothing wrong with organized evangelistic events. But with all the events we have carried out, it seems to us that the results have proven fairly minimal. Perhaps we have missed something. Jesus said, *"Let your light so shine before men, that they may see your good works and glorify your Father in heaven"* (Matt 5:16 NKJV). Notice here that it is the good works that radiate the light. Peter teaches this principle when he writes, *your conduct among the heathen should be so good that . . . they will have to recognize your good deeds and so praise God* (1 Pet 2:12 GNB).

The good works both practical and spiritual are the recognizable conduct of a believer. Peter goes on to explain God's purpose in calling His people to good works. *For God wants you to silence the ignorant talk of foolish people by the good things you do* (1 Pet 2:15 GNB). Even if they reject the message we bring, the way we help them, the way we treat them, the way we love them, the way we pray over them, the way we release healing on them all have an impact that our words alone could not bring. *If any of them do not believe God's word, your conduct will win them over to believe* (1 Pet 3:1 GNB).

In September 2010, Ed and Melissa took some of the members of Dayspring Church out on a Treasure Hunt. Kevin Dedmon wrote the book on this and we have found that Treasure Hunts are a great way to activate the body in hearing God and helping people. A few of their clues that evening included a bicycle, railroad tracks, a park bench, blue, white hair, right elbow and ankle. They went to the old train station, but there were not any park benches there. They decided to go to a local park where they knew there were some train tracks. When they arrived, one of the team remembered that she had seen a pool, but had not written it down. As they headed for the pool they saw their treasure. Sitting on a park bench facing the pool was a man with white hair, blue jeans, blue plaid shirt, blue denim jacket, reading a book.

They approached him and learned his name was Wolf. Ed showed him the list with right elbow and ankle on it – and asked if any of the items applied to him. He said that 15 years ago he had injured his right ankle on the job and had trouble with it since then. They prayed for his ankle on the spot. Then they asked if there was anything else he needed prayer for. He told them he needed a bicycle (another item on the list!) to go to work. They prayed with him for the provision he needed then, as they were about to leave, Ed remembered that he had a bicycle at the church. So Wolf became the owner of a bicycle, a constant reminder that God cared about him.

DO IT FOR JESUS

As God's representatives, He wants us to treat those around us with unselfish love. Paul told Timothy, *...to be rich in good deeds* (1 Tim 6:18 NIV). He told the Ephesian church to do what they do as if they were doing it for the Lord, *...knowing that whatever good anyone does, he will receive the same from the Lord* (Eph 6:8 NKJV). Sometimes we get a little uneasy about the idea of being rewarded for doing the right thing, but Paul doesn't seem to have that problem. As long as our motive is doing it to honor and proclaim Jesus we should expect heaven to back us up. Jesus indicated the same thing when His disciples asked Him a question. . . . *"Lord, when did we see You hungry and feed You, or thirsty and give You drink"? And the King will answer and say to them, "Assuredly, I say to you, inasmuch as you did it to one of the least of these My brethren, you did it to Me"* (Matt 25:37, 40 NKJV). Loving our neighbor is deceptively simple. Just love the next person you meet. Help them, comfort them, pray for them and heaven will back you up.

CHAPTER 5

GOSPEL OF PEACE

UNLOCKING THE TRANSFORMING POWER OF PEACE

Michael and Andrea Brewer have served in Haiti as missionaries since just before the earthquake that devastated the nation in January 2010. During their preparations to leave the states, someone had given them a prophetic word that they were about to enter the most difficult season of their lives, but through it, they would reap a great harvest. They had several orphan children living with them when the earthquake hit, but God protected them in the dire circumstances that followed. The first three months after the quake were a blur of long hours consumed with finding food, water, fuel and shelter. However, in the midst of crisis they gained access to the hearts and lives of scores of people as God gave them extraordinary favor.

In the aftermath of the disaster God has opened a door for explosive church growth with over 450 churches planted to date, 250 of these have sprung up in just the last year. The model they use for planting churches is extraordinary. It focuses on finding a man of peace, reaching their family and establishing a simple church in their house. They do this with a combination of prayer walking, bible stories, praying for the sick and casting out demons, ultimately leading people into salvation and freedom. Read more about their extraordinary journey in their new book, *Pioneering Faith*.

They train the leaders in this church planting movement to tell stories. They do not present themselves as Christians but as storytellers who are followers of Jesus and have learned some important stories. In nations filled with witchcraft and idol worship, most people live keenly aware of the spiritual realm but have no real concept of the origin of the deities they worship. This leaves many unanswered questions in their minds just waiting for the truth. To meet this need their church planters focus on just ten stories designed to answer their questions. Starting with creation and ending with Pentecost, these stories trace the plan of redemption and purpose of God for His creation, eventually drawing the listener into relationship with Jesus.

Finding the person of peace takes on a number of forms, but usually, the storyteller will hang out at an appropriate place and ask questions of those who pass by. They ask first about the local beliefs and superstitions, and then they ask if the person would like to hear a story about how it all began. They will tell just the story of creation and the fall, and then ask if they would like their household to hear the story. If their answer is yes, they will follow them home, gather the family, and repeat the story of creation then add in a second, perhaps the account of the flood.

They will then pray for the sick and ask the family if at some point in the future they would like to invite their neighbors to hear the stories and to receive prayer for healing. This home then becomes the home of peace. A few days later they will come back and repeat the process adding in one new story with the wider gathering. Over the weeks they add in stories until those who gather are saved, healed and delivered.

From the beginning, they look for those that show any leadership potential and spend special time with them. They also ask early on if anyone knows of another village they think needs to hear the stories of Jesus and they will begin to visit that village just to pray and look for the man of peace who would open the door to this new territory.

ILLUSIVE PEACE

We are convinced the Brewer's story is duplicable and that a focus on peace will serve as one of the key marks of this next season of life in the body of

Christ as we move into awakening. But what does that look like? One has only to glance at the news to know that the world needs peace. We hear peace talked about, but the peace the world talks about is powerless. It's a peace that has very little to do with what God wants to bring to us.

Consequently, the world has a very limited view of peace! Even though they long for it, their efforts appear futile and the peace they long for remains illusive. Just watch the behavior of those who call for peace and we can quickly see the inconsistencies. Demonstrators march for peace. Activists resort to violence and destruction to get peace. Governments stockpile weapons and fight wars to maintain it. A peace maintained by force can be lost by force. However, the kingdom of God carries a peace no weapon can thwart.

Even though the world has such a perverted understanding of true peace, as individuals we were created with a desire to live at peace. People desperately search for inner peace through all manner of activities: drugs, alcohol, counseling and psychoanalysis, extreme thrills and adventure, yoga and weird religions. People are so desperate to find peace that they resort to almost anything to exorcise their inner turmoil and agitation. They live in a constant search for something to fill the void inside.

This hunger for peace is actually a God-given need. We were created in the image of the God of Peace. Since peace is in His nature, we would expect His creation to look for peace as a part of fulfilling His image. Into this search Jesus gives a promise, *Peace I leave with you; My peace I give you. I do not give to you as the world gives. Do not let your hearts be troubled and do not be afraid* (John 14:27 NIV). We have already seen that the peace the world gives is an unstable peace at best. It is a peace built on fear and mutual distrust. It is a peace that comes through force, power and might. We know from experience that this kind of peace proves fragile, broken with the slightest misstep. Jesus came to introduce a peace that is not like the world's peace. His peace does not come from the end of a gun barrel, but it comes at the foot of the cross. His peace comes to us through a total surrender and obedience to His Father's will.

The way that we are to live as believers is to remain completely at peace, no matter what's going on around us. But Jesus does not stop with an atmosphere of peace marking our life. From His life we see the power of peace at work advancing the kingdom of God. If we can understand how Jesus extended the kingdom, it will give us a pattern we can use. Specifically, finding and ministering to a man of peace would appear to be Jesus' model for outreach.

MAN OF PEACE

Peace is one of God's mechanisms for reaching the world around us. If we can live at peace when everybody else is in turmoil, people will ask the reason for our peace. An unsaved John Wesley was powerfully moved by the unshakable peace of the Moravians in the midst of a storm at sea. He later said this was a central turning point for him. When everybody panics over some virus mentioned on the news, we do not react or respond in fear because of the peace that lives in us. Something must happen in us to cause us to trust God at a deeper level so that we will not live in reaction, or respond like the world.

When Jesus began his ministry, He introduced the kingdom of peace, which accompanied His rule established here on the earth. He introduced a way of living vastly different than anyone had experienced. When Jesus confronted a sickness, He saw it as an opportunity for a display of His Father's glory. He did not worry about whose fault it was. He just wanted it gone. In about the third year of Jesus' ministry, His disciples had seen Him do amazing things, and now it was their turn. He called them together, gave them power and authority and sent them out (Luke 9:1).

They came back excited. They had seen Him do all kinds of cool stuff and now they had seen God work through them. They saw the effect of the authority and power they were given. Then Jesus chose 70 others and sent them out with a detailed description of what they were to do. Look at what He said, *"Whatever house you enter, first say, 'Peace be to this house'"* (Luke 10:5). Where do we start with our evangelistic message? Jesus started by releasing His peace. He understood that people wanted and needed peace. He knew that the God-designed nature of humanity hungers for peace. His description of how we start in evangelism is to bless others with peace.

GOSPEL OF PEACE

We understand Jesus' instructions here as a global command. Jesus' ministry on earth modeled the peace of the Kingdom of God invading earth. The Prince of Peace came to release His peace on the earth. His instructions to His disciples then and now were to speak peace to the perceived need of those in the world who do not yet know Him. They do not know Him, but they all want peace. The gospel we carry is the Gospel of peace. The good news we bring is that you can have what your heart desires – you can have peace!

DEFINING PEACE

In English, the word *peace* conjures up a fairly passive picture. When we think of peace we think of an absence of conflict or hostility. Or perhaps we imagine a personality free from internal and external strife. We generally define peace in terms of what is not, instead of what is! But the peace of scripture is not defined as the lack of conflict but as the presence of the Prince of Peace.

The Greek word for peace, *eirene*, means, "to make peace, to cultivate or keep peace, or to be a peacemaker." It primarily denotes a state of being, not a relationship or attitude. This means that no one has the power to steal your peace. The word *eirene* is translated in the Septuagint as *shalom*, so we can draw some of its meaning from this Hebrew word. *shalom* means, "security, safety and prosperity of every kind." Its primary root is wholeness, so *shalom* gives a sense of well-being, to be complete, to live well or to be sound. This kind of peace is the normal state of all things under Christ's Lordship. When someone says *shalom* to you, they do not mean, "I hope you don't get into any trouble." They mean "I hope you have all the highest good coming your way." No wonder peace is what we present first!

What if we wandered around our cities and blessed everyone we met with peace? Wouldn't that be fun? Sometimes our mechanisms for evangelism seem to have more to do with trying to get people lost by pointing out their sin, rather than releasing heaven's powerful peace. If we would focus on peace first, they would sense the presence and power of God and respond to the grace of God that they are sensing. Jesus' peace consisted of a release of His presence, as well as a test of receptiveness to His rule. *If a man of peace is there, your peace will rest on him; but if not, it will return to you* (Luke 10:6). Jesus' pattern for evangelistic outreach begins with releasing His peace and then watching how they respond.

45

The phrase "man of peace" literally means son of peace or a person inclined toward peace. A man of peace then is somebody receptive to peace, or somebody that is in a position to receive what you're releasing. In Matthew's account he adds the phrase, ...if the house is worthy (Matt 10:13). The idea here is not whether the person deserves our blessing. The word worthy used here means, to be in a position to receive and bring back into balance.[1] When heaven's peace touches them, how will they respond? When we release our peace, and the person receives it, it means that they are willing to bring their life into balance with the peace of God. Only then will our peace remain on them. This was Jesus' model for reaching people, by releasing His peace to change the atmosphere.

Our society today seems more desperate for peace than ever. It's easy for us to decide what people need, instead of meeting their need. The American Psychologist magazine reported that over the last four decades of research, the top two terminal values of the American public are "a world at peace" and "family security."[2] By terminal values they mean the deepest core needs that motivate people. We live in a nation where the internal drive of almost every-one we see is peace and family security. We have the peace they need. We have the God of Peace, and we have the right, the privilege and the authority to release the peace that's on us into the lives of those around us.

We believe we need to return to the model Jesus gave us and start where He started. All of our communities have people who care about their community – find them and engage them with the peace of God. Speak our blessing of peace out and if they receive it, it becomes theirs. The peace of God is contagious as it begins to move through a community. Jesus' model for outreach will prove just as effective today as the day He initiated it.

A SEASON OF PEACE

The Peace Church is one of the fastest growing churches in Brazil. Their growth can be attributed to their emphasis on finding a man of peace and then affecting their household. Once a year they close down all their programs for an eight-week period they call the "season of peace." For two weeks prior they challenge all the people to pair up in teams of two and find a home of peace. It must be the home of a non-Christian that does not already go to church that is willing to host an eight-week study. Everyone including the pastor and staff participates. The pastor who was telling me about their system told me he had asked his family doctor if he would let them come to his home. He agreed, and the pastor and his wife spent their season of peace in their doctor's house.

The first night, they told a story about what happens when Jesus visits a home, and they demonstrated the story by praying for the sick. At the end of the evening, they asked the doctor and his wife if they would like to invite some of their friends for the next week. The next week ten non-Christian friends of this doctor were at the house and they told another story about what happens when Jesus visits a home. Again they prayed for the sick and for any other needs the guests had. Over the next weeks they saw most of the guests healed, set free and receive Jesus as Lord and Savior. At the end of the eight weeks, they take all the groups away for a retreat weekend, where they walk them all through deliverance, baptism in water and baptism in the Holy Spirit. One church we visited had just had their retreat weekend where they ministered to over 1,000 new believers, who were then added to the church.

Every one of us knows people who are receptive to the peace of God. They might not be receptive to church, but they are receptive to being touched by God's peace. What if we would begin to release God's peace because we are walking in peace? It's easy to release what we are walking in. The peace in us can release through us to touch others. Let's let the peace of God released through the Holy Spirit work to draw their hearts to accept Jesus. We believe this is the pattern God asks us to use in this season of awakening.

With the brokenness of our society we find it easy to point out their sin, when what they really need is hope. If we focus on their sin, we will probably miss giving them access to the peace we carry. What if we started where Jesus started and released His power and presence? Condemnation is a poor representative of the gospel of peace. For a long time we have tried to reach people by condemning them enough that they feel lost, so we can get them saved. But God gives us the right to release the gospel of peace purchased through the blood of His Son. Those who knew no peace can now respond to

Him and know real peace because the gospel of peace has come. *Therefore, having been justified by faith, we have peace with God...* (Rom 5:1). Sin made us enemies with God – the Gospel of peace restores us as His friends. Peace, the ultimate expression of the goodness of God.

SALTY PEACE

How many messages have we heard on salt? Growing up in Africa, we used salt for all kinds of things. It's both a preservative and a disinfectant. It also has powerful cleansing and healing properties. When we think of salt in scripture it speaks of our affect on the world around us. Jesus also taught that the salt in our lives must be connected to peace. *Salt is good; but if the salt becomes unsalty, with what will you make it salty again? Have salt in yourselves, and be at peace with one another* (Mark 9:50). Look at this verse carefully, *have salt in yourselves and be at peace with one another.* When we use the expression "rub salt into a wound," it means we are making somebody's pain feel worse. A lot of evangelistic efforts are just that, rubbing salt into wounds. We need to have salt in ourselves, but bring peace into our interactions with people. Some Christians go around rubbing salt in wounds and forget to bring peace. **Have salt and be at peace!** It's Jesus' model for reaching our friends and neighbors.

Peace must accompany any manifestation of our outreach in the community. Wherever we go, in the grocery store, to the bank or the gas station, the life of God through us needs to release peace. God's peace is more powerful than we have imagined. His peace works deeper than any argument we can bring to people. Look at what James says, *And the seed whose fruit is righteousness is sown in peace by those who make peace* (Jas 3:18). When you sow peace into a situation, it has the power to produce righteousness.

When we sow peace into someone's life, we literally sow a seed into their lives, a seed that can germinate and become righteousness in their household. As we sow in peace, we will begin to see the harvest in a greater measure. Sometimes we get frustrated that people are not responding when perhaps we are not sowing the right kind of seed. We believe that He's calling on us to sow peace as a primary mechanism for reaching the lost. If we will, we will begin to see the fruit of peace.

Fruit is defined as a product of plant growth, which serves as the reproductive body of a seed plant. God has given us the liberty of demonstrating His life, and the goodness of God will draw them to repentance. Peace has reproductive power that produces righteousness as its fruit. But if we do not demonstrate peace as a product of the goodness of God, people are not going to be drawn to repentance. Our nation remains a non-Christian nation because the church has not demonstrated the goodness of God. We have too often demonstrated a religious and a legalistic form that has no peace and produces no righteousness. God is destroying that flawed foundation and He's bringing us back to a revelation of His goodness where, as believers, we have the right to release His peace into situations and circumstances.

If we want to release His peace into homes and lives, we will need to guard what we talk about. Be careful talking about the negative around us, focusing on the evil instead of the beauty of the kingdom. Tares grow like crazy, but the wheat is unbelievable. The maturing heads of wheat are just dripping with life ready to produce an incredible harvest. Yes, there are a few tares out there, but let us determine to take our eyes off them and back on to the harvest. Often the prophetic does not help with this because some would rather look at what's wrong instead of what's going on with the wheat.

The harvest is riper than ever. We can choose what we look at. If there is nothing happening where you are, then find the reports of what God is doing in the earth and live there. We will not be able to release peace unless we live in peace. We have a tendency to talk about all the stuff that's going on and all the things wrong with our government and it may be true. In fact, it is a mess. But the harvest! The ground swell of the movement of the presence and power of God goes beyond anything we've experienced in history. If we will live there, we will have a peace to release into people's lives. We will have a peace to release into homes. We will have something to give so they can receive a tangible touch from the presence of God. It's astounding!

THE GOSPEL OF PEACE

Paul develops the gospel of peace: *But now in Christ Jesus you who formerly were far off have been brought near by the blood of Christ. For He Himself is our peace, who made both groups into one and broke down the barrier of the dividing wall* (Eph 2:13,14). There are two walls that come down in Christ. The first is the enmity between God and repentant sinners. Jesus paid the price to destroy the wall of hostility between us and God. He is our peace through the blood of the cross and the incredible message of salvation. His blood on heaven's mercy seat has made us at peace with God. We are now His friends who can live with an awareness of His presence because there is no barrier. We are at peace with God and at peace with each other.

The second wall is the enmity between races and factions. In Christ all artificial divisions are broken down, allowing the gospel of peace to spread through society without limits. This peace provides the evangelistic mechanism of the gospel, spreading exponentially when the body of Christ becomes carriers of His peace.

When we begin to take His peace and release it, not everyone is going to accept it, but scripture says it does not get wasted. It just comes back to us. We do not always know what that looks like. All we can do is offer it, and if they do not receive it, the peace comes back to us so we can offer it somewhere else. The beauty of His peace is that there is always enough. The moment our offering of peace is accepted, there's more in our hand so we never run short of God's transforming peace.

Sandra, Farley and Kelly were at the state capitol, and while they were there, more than one hundred people disrupted the place for more than an hour. When they were thrown out of the Senate chamber, they began marching in the halls, carrying signs and banners. Fear and tension filled the place. When our team finally stopped to pray God's peace into the situation, all of the chanting stopped immediately and never resumed. Within moments, peace replaced fear – it was a dramatic and sudden change in atmosphere. (They did wonder why they had not prayed sooner.)

We want to challenge each one reading this chapter. Would you make it a point of releasing the peace of God into several situations this week? Walk into a place where there is a little bit of tension or conflict and just begin to release His peace. The Prince of Peace, Jesus, will invade the circumstances where there is no peace and cause our peace to be their portion, cause our peace to be a tangible part of the way they live their life. We bless you with the peace of God in Jesus' name.

CHAPTER 6

THINK LIKE HEAVEN

BREAKING OFF LIMITATIONS OF THE NATURAL MIND

In the afternoon session in Delhi, a local Assembly of God pastor and his wife came to the meeting desperate for healing. That morning I had given a testimony of blind eyes being opened, and someone had called this pastor and invited them to come. The wife had lost the vision in her right eye and her son had developed the same hereditary condition, completely losing the eyesight in his right eye.

I started by praying for the mother and after the first prayer she was able to see light and make out the faces around her but they were still fuzzy. I prayed again and this time she could see those close around her, but her distance vision was still blurry. I wanted to pray for her a third time but she was so concerned for her son that she asked me to pray for him next. Instead of me praying, I asked her to lay her hands on her son and pray for his eye to open. She did, and prayed a wonderful petition prayer, begging God to heal him. When she had finished, we checked his eyesight but nothing changed.

I asked her to pray again, but this time to pray with authority as a daughter of the King and command the blind eye to open in Jesus' name. She went for it and when we checked his eye out, the son was able to count the number of fingers held up right in front of him. We celebrated, and then I asked her to pray again the same way. This time when we checked his eye after the prayer, the son could count the fingers held up from 20 feet away. The mother broke down and wept for joy! When she had composed herself, I asked her to check out her own eyesight and to her delight, she realized she could see perfectly both up close and at a distance. We are in relationship with a wonderful Father who loves His children.

DEMONSTRATIONS OF POWER

God designed miracles to break through the limits of the natural mind and cause people to reexamine their belief structure. I once heard an evangelist refer to miracles as the dinner bell for salvation. From the inception of the church, signs and wonders have been in evidence. Although through many periods of church history they seem few and far between, if we look at the historical record with an open mind, we will discover that they have never ceased.

For those of us who look to the reformation for our spiritual roots we recognize that some of the church fathers spoke against miracles as a normative part of church life. The reformers struggled with the miracles that were evident in their day in part because the Catholic Church pointed to the miracles within their structure as the validation of their doctrine. Even today, one of the marks they look for in bestowing sainthood is that the person must have at least a couple of confirmed miracles.

Because the reformers were challenging some of the Catholic's doctrinal positions, it seemed right to Luther and others to attack the validity of the miraculous. This single decision has radically affected the evangelical church for centuries. We know for a fact that Luther believed in healing, because he prayed for his own friend, Melanchthon, who was gravely ill and he was healed.[1] If only they had grasped the fact that the miracles are simply expressions of the goodness of God and not the validation of right doctrine. Today we live with the benefit of healing ministries that have paved the way to see the miraculous restored to the church.

During the 1950's healing movement, healing was primarily seen as a platform ministry. Then during the Jesus movement, many in the body began to be activated as they learned to pray for one another. When John Wimber came on the scene in the 80s, he established the theology for healing as a function of body ministry. I remember being at a conference with Ian Andrews in the mid 80s. We were experiencing a substantial outpouring of the gifts of healing and words of knowledge. We saw some incredible healings, but most happened as we ministered from the platform. The longing of our heart was to see the whole body activated, but it seemed out of reach. One morning toward the end of the meetings Ian came downstairs and told us he had a dream concerning the future of the healing movement. It depicted the body of Christ waking up to do the works of Jesus with a mountain of men and women, all doing the ministry of healing.

Now years later we live in the season of fulfillment, as God pours out the anointing for signs and wonders across His body, the church. The body ministry component of this move of the Spirit means that the main activity of the church will happen in and through the people of God living a naturally supernatural lifestyle, outside of church events. Meetings in the building will celebrate what He's doing out in society. It is a moment of glorious fulfillment of the equipping that is on God's heart. We live in one of the most important transitions in human history - a season when everything that God has promised is being released into the body. For the church to accept this requires a substantial mind shift. The people of God must make the move from passively receiving to actively participating in the work of ministry. We must begin to see through heaven's perspective.

CHANGING MINDS

Let's look at a passage of scripture that deals with this change of mindset. The story of the Paralytic being healed in the book of Luke starts with a room full of skeptical people. The text says that *teachers of the law sitting by, who had come out of* **every** *town of Galilee, Judea, and Jerusalem* (Luke 5:17 NKJV). Let yourself step into the scene for a few minutes. The house was packed with religious people who struggled to believe. They had come because of what they had heard, but these miraculous stories had been filtered through their religious history. Jesus had not met any of their expectations of who the Messiah would be; this filled the room with questions. In the midst of a skeptical crowd we read *that the power of the Lord was present to heal* (Luke 5:17 NKJV). God is going to do a kingdom demonstration. When we understand kingdom culture, we realize that the **more difficult the circumstance, the more powerful the potential for encounter.**

It is no wonder that when the friends arrived with the paralytic, they couldn't get anywhere near Jesus. Their only option was an act of both love and desperation; they tore a hole in the roof and got their friend to Jesus.

When Jesus saw the paralytic in front of Him, He knew the friends saw the need for healing, but Jesus is aware of another need and responded in a way no one had imagined. What He did scandalized the crowd but set the man up to receive his full deliverance: *Friend, your sins are forgiven you* (Luke 5:20).

POWER VS. AUTHORITY

Immediately the religious crowd went nuts and began to ask each other, ... *Who can forgive sins but God alone?* (Luke 5:21). The word "can" used in this statement is a derivative of *dunimus* the word for power. Essentially, they asked who has the power to forgive sins except God?

Jesus answered their question about power with a declaration of His authority. *"But, so that you may know that the Son of Man has authority on earth to forgive sins,"—He said to the paralytic—"I say to you, get up, and pick up your stretcher and go home"* (Luke 5:24). He let them know that He did not just have the power to forgive sins; He had the right to exercise the power both to forgive and to heal. We will look in depth at the distinction and source of power and authority in the next chapter.

After the paralytic was healed, there was a mixed response from the crowd that had gathered. The text says that *They were all seized with astonishment and began glorifying God and they were filled with fear, saying "we have seen remarkable things today"* (Luke 5:26). What a reaction; even in their amazement they glorify God. They were giving praise to God for what they had seen but in the act of praise something else happens.

SOAKED WITH FEAR

It says they glorified God and they were filled with fear. What's that about? The actual word "filled" here also means soaked. They were literally soaked with fear. Have you ever been soaked in fear? Something happened in the act of the miracle that challenged what they thought, believed and understood. We can react in different ways to a miracle. Some rejoice, while others react by doubting that it even happened. The religious leaders here responded with fear because they had encountered the unknown. In this case, their preconceived ideas were being challenged and the response was fear. Fear is the human response to a perceived threat. Though fear intends to keep us safe, it actually puts us in danger by clouding our thinking process.

OUT OF OUR MIND

Something else is going on that explains the fear even further. It says *they were all seized with astonishment* (Luke 5:26.) The Greek word used here actually means, "the throwing of the mind out of its normal state."[2] What they had witnessed messed with their thinking. The natural mind could not reconcile what they had witnessed with what they knew to be true. The tension this created made them crazy. They couldn't process what they had seen because it challenged their understanding. How many of us have been there? A propensity exists in every one of us to rely on the natural realm. This dependence on the natural can make it hard for us to access and live from the supernatural realm. This was the dilemma for the religious leaders. They were caught in the natural realm and their response to their minds being thrown out of their normal state was to say, "We have seen extraordinary or remarkable things today."

They had seen something that was outside of their experience and it had messed with their mind. They simply did not know how to process what they had just witnessed. We all must deal with this dilemma. We need to shift our mindset so that we can think in a new way about what God is doing, learning to think from heaven rather than from earth.

This is what Paul told the Corinthians; he wrote to the church, not to unbelievers when he said, *A natural man does not accept the things of the Spirit of*

God (1 Cor 2:14). The natural mind just could not accept that paralytics walk because it seemed foolish. Why? Because they had not seen it before. It was not in their experience and consequently not in their understanding. It is only understood when it is appraised spiritually. My natural mind cannot reason out a way to get paralytics to walk. We've got to get over into the mind of the Spirit. We've got to access heaven's way of thinking. We've got to access that "other realm", the spiritual realm. We must reach beyond the natural and believe that heaven always wants to heal because healing is in God's nature.

THE PARADOX

The word "extraordinary" that the teachers of the law used to describe their experience is the word paradoxa. The Greek word means contrary to our experience and we get our English word paradox from the same root word. It means a situation, person or a thing that combines contradictory features. In other words, this was not matching what they thought might happen. It is a situation made up of opposites that seem impossible and yet are actually possible. In the natural realm, paralytics do not walk. But in the spiritual realm, paralytics always walk. In the natural realm, it seems unreasonable to assume that a paralytic will get up and walk. That's the natural mind. But when we approach a paralytic from a spiritual mindset, it would be normal for the paralytic to get up and walk. When we operate from the spiritual realm, the impossible becomes normal. That's the paradox.

The disciples and the crowd milling around were gripped by the paradox. Their natural mind could not wrap around what God had done in a moment. It did not make sense. It was outside their expectation. As believers today we need a revelation of heaven that brings resolve to the paradox. We've got to get out of our natural mind and into the supernatural mind. Otherwise, we are not going to be able to understand what God does in this hour. More than that, our goal is not just to understand it, we must be able to participate in what He is doing in the earth. Otherwise, we will forever be uncomfortable, filled with fear, standing on the sidelines wondering what is happening.

Farley met a homeless lady on the street. She sat dejectedly on a curb, unable, in her high heels and slightly drunk condition, to pull her suitcase up a hill. She had hopelessness and despair written all over her. He sat next to her on the curb, feeling awkward and unspiritual, at a loss for what to say. He told her about Jesus and how much God loves her, and then pulled her suitcase up the hill for her, all the while worried what those driving past might think. After maybe ten minutes of sharing God's love with her, she still felt utterly hopeless.

Just before Farley left her, he discovered that she had fallen three weeks before and had injured her shoulder. When he asked if he could pray for her, she replied, "Sure, but it won't do any good." She felt like she was far beyond the reach of God's goodness. Why would He even bother with someone like me? I have screwed up my life beyond all hope.

After Farley prayed, a shocked look came over her face. As she rotated her arm, she found to her amazement that God had healed her. A few minutes later she gave her life to Jesus. She was visibly shaken by the goodness of God. Joy and hope began to rise in her. Where nothing else seemed to help, the power of God's amazing goodness broke through.

THINK LIKE HEAVEN

When we begin to think like heaven, we learn to expect divine intervention. The impossible finally begins to feel normal. We do not look at sickness with fear. We look at it with expectancy, knowing that it provides an opportunity for God to pour out His Spirit. It is an opportunity for His glory to get released into this realm. God wants to fundamentally change the way we think. If we are honest, we all struggle with this paradox. It does not matter how many miracles we have seen, there is still a struggle because our history has not taught us that paralytics always walk. In fact, our experience tells us that it does not happen very often. "God, open our eyes to see sickness as You see it."

There was a fascinating interchange between the disciples and Jesus in John's Gospel. They encountered a man who was born blind and they came to Jesus with a question. *Who sinned, this man or his parents, that he would be born blind* (John 9:2)? In other words, whose fault was it? What excuse could we have for this blind man not getting healed? It's what they were asking. Why? It's a blame response that removes us from the responsibility of changing that situation. If there is a bad reason, then we are not responsible for doing anything about it. Now, look at Jesus' answer. What does He say? It was neither. It had nothing to do with who sinned, but rather, ... *that the works of God should be revealed in him* (John 9:3).

Jesus looked at a blind man and He saw the blindness as an opportunity for the release of healing power. He was demonstrating His view of sickness. He looked at sickness as an opportunity for the display of God's glory. Oh, if we would really get this, we would wander through the malls looking for anyone with a limp. We would be actively praying for anyone sick in our workplace. We would do it because we are starting to live in the supernatural realm - a realm where it is normal for paralytics to walk, for the blind to see and the deaf to hear.

When we begin to take hold of this, something changes in the way we view sickness. Something changes in the way we view a circumstance. God wants to release His glory into the earth and He wants to do it through us. He wants to transform our mindset so that we think like He thinks, so we can begin to do what He did.

IN THE PRESENCE OF THE GLORY

Go back to our Luke 5:26 verse just for a minute. *They were seized with astonishment and began glorifying God. They were filled with fear saying, "We've seen remarkable things today."* We would encourage everybody to look up that word "remarkable" because there's another layer that we need to touch. The Greek word used here is *paradoxa*. It is a compound word combining the prefix *para*, which means "in the presence of or to come near" and *doxa,* which means "glory". When they said we have seen remarkable things today, they were inferring that they had been in the presence of the glory or that they had come near the glory. When we get into the presence of the glory, paralytics always walk because that's what happens in the paradox. You may have two things that do not seem like they are true, but when you push far enough they become true. How do the natural mind and the spiritual mind come together? It comes together when we are in the presence of the glory.

When we get in the presence of the glory, God begins to release His glory through us at a level that we've not seen or understood before. This increase in His presence changes the way we view situations and circumstances. We will no longer look from a natural perspective but from heaven's point of view. We believe this shift has begun across the Body of Christ, not just in our church, but also in the city and in our nation. This shift of expectancy will cause every member of the Body of Christ to walk into their workplace with the expectation that God heals, that He delivers, that He saves and that He does wonders. He is doing it today!

Let's be honest for a moment. How many of us tend to live tied to what we have not yet experienced way too much of the time? Yet God is calling us to the other side of the paradox. He's calling us to live in the presence of the glory, to be so full of Him that when we walk out into society, we go as carriers of glory. When we are full of His presence the glory naturally leaks out of us and people get touched, healed and saved. Prophetic words and words of knowledge are released. People encounter the goodness of God because we are living in the presence of the glory and we never step out of it. We refuse to let our natural mind be the limiter. We refuse to let the paradox mess with us.

Do we have questions? We have a big box of questions. We join Randy Clark in calling it our "Mystery Box." You would not believe how many things are in our mystery box. Many of you know that Sally has struggled with her hearing for years, but despite her own struggle, she had her first deaf-from-birth ears opened several months ago. She stood in front of this person who had never heard a sound, and the enemy screamed in her ear, "You can't hear; you don't have the right to pray." What's happening? The natural mind tends to accept the limitation because it is reasonable, but she chose to let that voice stir faith. If the accuser is saying I can't, that must mean it's going to happen. Suddenly she is living on the other side of the paradox; the moment she laid hands on his ears they opened. Why? Because in the spiritual realm, deaf ears just can't stay deaf.

Ask the Holy Spirit right now to open your mind. Say, "God, I have trouble with this because I do not see paralytics walking yet, but I know there is more. My rational mind gets in the way of that because of my limited experience.

God help me to see the way You see and move me to a place of expectancy." Something is changing in the way we think and look at the circumstance. God is moving us into an expectancy of living in the realm of the supernatural as a normal part of the way we live. Are you hungry for that? I'm desperate. I'm desperate to live and walk by the Spirit in a greater and greater measure.

CHAPTER 7

POWER & AUTHORITY

EQUIPPING THE BODY TO DO THE WORKS OF JESUS

Jeremy, one of the young men in our church, grew up with dyslexia. By the time he was in the sixth grade, he could barely read on a third grade reading level. The school planned to hold him back from the seventh grade. Over the summer, his parents got him a tutor. She taught him to read, but it was all for show. Even though he could pronounce the words, he still was unable to comprehend what he read.

One evening in November 2011 as Bill Johnson ministered at Dayspring Church, Bill had a word of knowledge for learning disorders. Jeremy, who was operating one of the cameras, responded and people around him began to pray. The moment they laid hands on him, he felt like someone put defibrillator paddles on either side of his head, releasing a pulse of electricity that caused his whole body to jump. Then Bill asked people to do what they could not do before, so he picked up his manual from the conference, and for the first time in his life read and understood what he read. It was a glorious testimony of God's power.

Two years after his healing, Jeremy went on a mission trip to Oaxaca, Mexico with Sally and me. We helped an orphanage build a building and ministered in a conference in the evenings. During the Sunday morning service, I asked the team to release some words of knowledge and Jeremy felt he heard "learning disorders." Instantly the enemy started trying to intimidate him, but he had made a declaration to not be silent. He released the word, and I shared his testimony and gave the altar call. Twenty children with learning disability came to his line, and as he released the healing that he had received, fifteen of the children testified that they could read and comprehend better than before. Jeremy now walks in a new identity that comes with a new authority!

A few months later Jeremy went with us to Lebanon. Again he had the opportunity to share his testimony at a conference. God touched many, healing them of shame and the inability to learn. One woman struggled with Attention Deficit Disorder and as she received prayer, she felt an electric shock in her head. She said instantly she received clarity and received peace in her mind. Jeremy's testimony today is that the only thing he has found more life-changing than receiving his healing has been God giving him the opportunity to release it to others.

THE BAPTISM OF JESUS

At His baptism heaven opened over Jesus and the Father confirmed the identity of His Son. The Father's declaration established that Jesus would speak with the authority of heaven. The Holy Spirit then descended on Him with the power for ministry. Jesus, as the Son of Man full of the Holy Spirit, preached and ushered in the Kingdom of God. His authority and power were demonstrated as He destroyed the works of the evil one, healing the sick, casting out demons and raising the dead. In His life here on earth, Jesus demonstrated heaven's power and authority. The more we identify ourselves with Him, the more His power and authority reside in us.

Once He had modeled a life of power and of authority, Jesus was ready to send out the disciples as a continuation of His ministry. He called the twelve together and gave them power and authority (Luke 9:1). In other words, He commissioned them to go out and do exactly what He had been doing. To accomplish this they would need both the power to do the work and the authority to exercise the power.

RIGHT AND ABILITY

Now before we go further let us look at some definitions. Most dictionaries define authority in terms of power. A quick search of various sources shows that they all include power in their definition and most list power as a synonym for authority. However, while they may appear synonymous, there is a clear distinction. The Oxford Dictionary defines *authority* as "the power or **right** to give orders, make decisions and enforce obedience." The same dictionary lists the definition of power as "the **ability** or capacity to do something or act in a particular way". *Authority* is the **right** to do something while *power* is the **ability** to do it. Though closely linked, we need both power and authority to do the work of God.

If you find my car keys on the table, you can use them to take my car and go anywhere you want. With the keys in hand, you have the power to drive my car. Having the keys in your hand gives you what you need to make the car operate. But unless I gave you permission to take the keys, you do not have the authority or right to operate my vehicle. If I give you the keys, you have the full package. Jesus said to Peter, *"I will give you the keys of the kingdom of heaven"* (Matt 16:19). In Scripture the word *key* is generally understood to represent a symbol of power and authority. To accomplish the task of executing the will of God here on earth, we need both the power of the Holy Spirit and the authority of the commission.

Jesus made the distinction in the story about the healing of the paralytic man in Capernaum (discussed in the last chapter). Four friends brought the man to the home where Jesus was, but when they arrived, it was so crowded that they could not get in. They took him up on the roof, made a hole and let him down in front of Jesus. When Jesus saw their faith He responded in a way no one had imagined. S*on, your sins are forgiven* (Mark 2:5). Immediately, the religious crowd was offended and began to ask each other, *…Who can forgive sins but God alone?* (Mark 2:7). The word *can* in this statement is *dunatai*, which means, "to be capable of" and is derived from *dunamis* the Greek word power. Essentially, they are asking one another, who has the power to forgive sins?

Jesus, knowing their thoughts, gave a stunning answer. *"But in order that you may know that the son of Man has authority on earth to forgive sins,"* He told the paralytic, *"I say to you rise, take up your pallet and go home"* (Mark 2:10). What an answer; He answered their question about **power** with a declaration of His authority - I don't just have the power to forgive sins, I have the **right** to exercise the power. For Jeremy, the power of God touched him when he was healed. But when he broke through the condemnation and released it to others, he stepped into a place of authority. He walks today in the power of the Spirit and in the authority of his identity as a child of the King.

Jesus demonstrated the crucial difference between having power that gives us the ability to do the works of God and having the authority, which gives us the right to exercise the power that we have been given. To have the confidence to step out of our comfort zone and take the risk to begin to demonstrate the kingdom, we need the authority of heaven behind us. Before we go further with authority let us make sure we understand that the source of authority is the commission. Christ's commission of the disciples and our commission to advance the kingdom came with the authority necessary to complete the task. But the source of the power we need comes from an encounter with the Holy Spirit.

THE POWER

The Greek word used in scripture for power is *dunamis* from which we get our English word dynamite. It means "having the capability of might." Power is a manifestation of God's presence. When the presence of the Lord comes in the form of the Holy Spirit, the world will see mighty works. Jesus promised His disciples that they would receive power from the Holy Spirit (Acts 1:8). This power would also produce a tremendous evangelistic thrust as the rule of God invades this present evil age.

One of the challenges the church faces is the tendency to believe that we have received all that we are to get. As Baptists, Sally and I had no expectation of ever getting more than what we received at salvation. And the same unfortunately can apply for many Pentecostals who believe that because they spoke in tongues, they have it. Our religious history makes it difficult to believe there is more. Tragically, when we make a single gift our measure of the baptism in the Holy Spirit, it falls far short of the biblical measure. You shall receive power!

When Paul tells the Ephesians, *do not be drunk with wine,… but be filled with the Spirit* (Eph 5:18), there is an interesting twist to the verse. The phrase "be filled" is the present continuous tense of the verb, which could translate as, "be being filled." This would seem to promise that there is more if we want it. We are to be continually filled with the Holy Spirit, meaning that there is always more.

Paul surely believed in "more" when he wrote toward the end of his ministry, *That I may know him and the power of his resurrection* (Phil 3:10). We see the apostle hungry for more of the power that comes from intimacy with the Lord. To know Him is one of the works of the Spirit. If we live in the Spirit, we will come to know Him more and know His will. If Paul was still praying for more, then we are certainly in good company when we stay hungry for more of His presence and power.

POWER ENCOUNTER

The power we need comes from one source, an encounter with the Holy Spirit. Several years ago I felt I heard the Lord say that our son Philip was to step into the ministry alongside us and lead the body of Dayspring Church at least for a season. Philip has an incredible pastoral heart and literally became the pastor at the airline where he worked. He received the baptism of the Holy Spirit when he was very young and occasionally got in trouble for his bold witness. Having been a missionary's kid and a pastor's kid, he had seen enough ill treatment that had come our way at times that he really was not sure that it was what he should be doing.

Toward the end of 2011, we hosted Randy Clark's Kingdom Foundations Conference at Dayspring Church. Before the conference as I prepared, I felt a strong impression that Philip was about to receive an impartation. The conference was incredible with many miracles and great times of impartation. It was during this same conference that Jeremy received his dramatic healing. Although we had experienced a glorious time I felt a little disappointed. Throughout the conference, Philip had carried the burden of serving. He helped with sound and served as tech support wherever needed. He received prayer a couple of times but I knew there was more.

The day after the conference ended I sat in my office and began to talk to the Father about the future, sharing my disappointment. As I prayed I heard the Holy Spirit tell me to take Philip up to Pennsylvania for the "Empowered" conference that Randy was holding in their facility in Mechanicsburg, PA. Philip was free so we set off the next morning. We had a wonderful time connecting with Randy and his team and thoroughly enjoyed a week away together. But then we came to the last night of the meetings and again we had had a lot of fun together and had helped minister, but there had been no real encounter.

Just before the offering that night I heard the Holy Spirit speak again and this time He had a question for me. How badly do you want Me to touch your son? My response was immediate, anything you say I will do! What happened next is outside my understanding and is in no way a theological statement. It was pure obedience. I heard the Holy Spirit say put $1000 in the offering. I did not have a checkbook or that much cash so I wrote out a credit card slip for the thousand.

A few minutes later they took the offering and the moment my envelope hit the bucket, the Holy Spirit hit Philip who was sitting next to me. He slid to the floor and went under the chair in front of him and the power of God rested on him the remainder of the meeting. I had great difficulty getting him out to the car and had even more trouble getting him up to the motel room. That night he never made it to his bed, he crawled around on the floor laughing, crying, repenting, and then laughing some more. All night he made declarations of the awe and majesty of Jesus his Lord.

I finally went to sleep about 2 a.m. and left him in the capable hands of the Holy Spirit. When I woke in the morning, he was halfway up on his bed worshiping Jesus. When we arrived home the next day people immediately saw the change. His passion for the presence of God increased dramatically and whenever he would begin to minister, the prophetic flowed like a river. He came on staff that year and served for three years before he stepped into his current role as lead pastor of Dayspring. He entered this season of his destiny with an encounter and impartation more powerful than any I have yet received.

GOSPEL OF POWER

The gospel message must include demonstration. Paul told the Thessalonians that the gospel message he brought came not *…in word only, but also in power and in the Holy Spirit and with full conviction* (1 Thess 1:5). He wanted them to understand that the way he presented the gospel provided the pattern they should use as they spread the good news. He told the Corinthians the same thing, *And my message and my preaching were not in persuasive words of wisdom, but in demonstration of the Spirit and of power, so that your faith would not rest on the wisdom of men, but on the power of God* (1 Cor 2:4,5).

Healing and miracles demonstrate the Spirit's power. The Holy Spirit demonstrates the validity of the word preached. God wants people's faith to be built on both the Word of God and the testimony of His healing power. It is our responsibility to give the Holy Spirit some risk to work with. If we play it safe, we give Him no opportunity to validate the message. Jesus said, *… "the Spirit of truth who goes out from the Father, he will testify about me. And you also must testify…"* (John 15:26-27 NIV). We testify with our words, and when we step out and give Him opportunity, the Spirit testifies to the truth of our message with power.

Paul also deals with the fear of miracles. Growing up, I was often warned about miracles. They cautioned that, "We don't want people trusting in the wrong things." But in 1 Corinthians 2:5 Paul states that he wants their faith founded in the power of God and not just in good arguments. Doctrine is established when we see the same truth presented repeatedly. Writing to the Romans, Paul speaks in irrefutable terms; *in the power of (attesting miracles) signs and wonders, in the power of the Spirit; so that from Jerusalem and round about as far as Illyricum I have fully preached the gospel of Christ* (Rom 15:19). This means that the gospel is not fully preached until it is demonstrated. A powerless church preaches a diluted gospel message.

THE AUTHORITY

In the great commission, Jesus described the limitless extent of His authority with the words; *All authority has been given to Me in heaven and on earth* (Matt 28:18). As a result of His death and resurrection, all authority in the universe belongs to Him. The cross-stripped any authority the enemy had stolen from man or any other realm, and it ALL now rests on the conquering Lamb, King Jesus.

Then, after commissioning His followers to make disciples in every nation, He made a solemn promise to them that *I am with you always, even to the end of the age* (Matt 28:20). His staggering promise is that, as we walk in obedience to heaven's mandate to make disciples of the nations, He is present with us and in us always. Catch the connection. All authority in the universe belongs to Jesus and He is with us. By implication then, all authority in the entire universe is resident and available to us.

In His commission, He delegated to us the authority to act on His behalf as we do His work. Literally, a power-of-attorney transaction, written in His blood, authorizes us to represent Him in extending His kingdom rule here on the earth. As His ambassadors, we carry out His instructions by bringing heaven's rule into this realm. We are to do it just like He did it by exercising His power and authority, healing the sick, casting out demons, raising the dead and preaching the good news.

A MAN UNDER AUTHORITY

One day a centurion came to Jesus asking for healing for his servant (Matt 8:5). But when Jesus offered to go home with him to heal the servant, he did not want to trouble Jesus. As a soldier he understood authority. He knew that when he gave an order it was followed. He saw something in Jesus that he recognized as obedience to a higher authority and knew that Jesus only needed to speak a word for it to happen (Matt 8:8).

The centurion understood something about authority and Jesus related it to faith. He recognized what happens when someone walks in true authority. Jesus made note of this and declared it the greatest faith He had seen in all

Israel (Matt 8:10). Then He told him to go home, because what he had believed for had happened. The power of the Spirit needs the authority of our commission for us to do the things Jesus asks us to do.

To explore the connection between authority and faith think about the faith required to speak with authority. It requires risk to declare what God is going to do – the reason why faith and risk are so closely linked. We have authority because of our identity as sons and daughters of the King. This authority gives us the power of attorney to use the name of Jesus, but we do not step into our authority without faith. We must take the risk to speak in His name and expect Him to attest His word.

Back to Jeremy's story for a moment, the power encounter at his healing stirred in him a desire to see others set free. But his breakthrough did not come until he took a risk and shared his word of knowledge. The moment he took the risk and stepped out, he moved into a new realm of authority, and healing for others with similar conditions began to manifest through him. When we understand our authority as believers we will learn to take the risk of faith and begin to declare what God is about to do. There is a direct connection between authority and faith.

POTENTIAL FOR ACTION

The Greek word for authority is *exousia* - the "right, permission or freedom in a legal sense; the right to do something or the right over something, distinct from intrinsic ability, but conveys the definite possibility of action."[1] Notice that the definition of the Greek word makes the same distinction that we did earlier between right and ability. Authority is the right to do something or the right over something while power is the ability, which comes from an empowering by the Spirit.

We also particularly like the idea of "the definite possibility of action" in this definition. There is a potential of action implied in authority. When we understand our authority we become walking encounters, looking for a place to make a deposit of the Kingdom of God. Every moment of the day in every situation we have the potential of the love and power of God being released through us. All it takes is risk, stepping out in faith and allowing the deposit of His presence that is in us to begin to flow through us. The more we walk in our authority, the greater the potential for breakthrough.

The death of Christ broke the power of Satan's authority (an authority stolen in the fall) and with it any legal hold he had over us. Paul tells believers that *… He rescued us from the domain of darkness, and transferred us to the kingdom of His beloved Son* (Col 1:13). He delivered us from the authority or kingdom of darkness and brought us in under the rule of Christ. He has also transferred us into His domain to live under His authority as sons and daughters with the right to exercise His power with His authority.

If this authority is to function properly, we must remain under authority as Christ lived under the authority of His Father. As a man accustomed to giving and receiving orders, the Centurion recognized this same characteristic in Jesus. The more we step into our authority, the more dependent we become on our relationship with Jesus and our intimate fellowship with Him. Only then will we instinctively know His wishes and carry out His will here on earth.

We see the relational component of authority emphasized by Jesus when the disciples came back amazed that the demons were subject to them in His name.

> *The seventy returned with joy, saying, "Lord, even the demons are subject to us in your name." And He said to them, "I was watching Satan fall from heaven like lightning. Behold, I have given you authority to tread on serpents and scorpions, and over all the power of the enemy, and nothing will injure you. Nevertheless do not rejoice in this, that the spirits are subject to you, but rejoice that your names are recorded in heaven." (Luke 10:17-20)*

Jesus celebrates their revelation and release of authority, and then He brings them back to the source. Rejoice that you have been brought back into relationship with your heavenly Father because He is the source.

Lest we think in any way that this was a caution against using our authority, look at Jesus' personal response when they used the authority and exercised the power to bring down Satan's strongholds. *At that very time He rejoiced greatly in the Holy Spirit...* (Luke 10:21). Let this image fill your mind, Jesus rejoicing in the Spirit because His disciples were beginning to get it. They began to walk in the authority He had given them. The same applies to us today. Every time we step out in the power and authority we possess, heaven rejoices.

CHAPTER 8

SIGNS & WONDERS

RESTORING MIRACLES TO THE GOSPEL MESSAGE

One evening in a church meeting in Sao Paulo, Brazil, after a short message I asked anyone in the room who needed healing to stand. About a third of those in the room stood, but one man could not stand. Max, a young man in his late 20's had been a cripple from birth. As everyone stood, Sally looked over at Max and felt a deep stirring of faith for his healing. So she walked over to him looked him in the eye and said to him, "Stand up." He responded immediately and stood to his feet. Then she said, "come" and with some of the team helping him, he began to walk with shuffling steps toward the front.

Only when he began to give his testimony did we realize the extent of the miracle we had just witnessed. Max was born with no feeling below the waist and had never been able to move his legs, much less walk. He told us that he had spent most of his young life on a bed until eventually he learned to get around, using crutches by swinging his legs and torso forward. The moment Sally told him to stand, he said he felt electricity go through him and he began to feel his legs for the first time in his life. Then, when she told him to come, he realized as he went to take his first step that he could move and control his legs. He was one happy man!

A short time later, when I gave the invitation for salvation, Max was on his feet again and one of the first to "walk" to the front to give his life to Jesus. And he was not alone. That night as many responded to the goodness of God they had witnessed and came forward to give their lives to Jesus. Scripture really is true. The goodness of God does draw men and women to repentance (Rom 2:4). It is the goodness of God that made a way for our salvation and it is the goodness of God that heals our bodies, heals our minds and heals our emotions. The goodness of God breaks through darkness and despair, drawing hearts and minds into His glorious salvation.

GOD TESTIFYING WITH US

The writer of Hebrews describes this connection between miracles and the Gospel message. He assures us that when we step out in faith, heaven responds. *God also testifying with them, both by signs and wonders and by various miracles and by gifts of the Holy Spirit according to His own will* (Heb 2:4). We would suggest based on this promise, that normal Christian life should be 'God testifying with us.' As believers we should have a life punctuated by God's testimony, through signs, wonders, miracles and gifts of the Holy Spirit. For our life to be marked by the supernatural all that He requires of us is a willingness to step out and take the risk.

The context of this verse is crucial because it cautions us not to neglect our great salvation. The first few verses of this chapter give a warning (Heb. 2:1-3). The writer tells us to pay careful attention to the things we have heard so they do not slip away. This means that it is possible for us to inadvertently drift away from a truth that belongs to us. We believe that this is the case when it comes to healing. Healing belongs to us, but over the centuries, we have drifted away, even to the point of preaching against it.

The final warning, spoken by the Lord and confirmed to us is chilling, *how shall we escape if we neglect so a great salvation* (Heb 2:3 NKJV). Jesus established the direct connection between healing and the gospel message. The warning here is real. Do not water down the foundation that Jesus put in place. God did not start us out and then leave us to do it on our own. He intends to testify with us as we proclaim His word. It is so easy for us to let experience dictate truth, rather than the Word setting our standard.

Much of the church has fallen into this trap and the result is a powerless message. This is precisely the shift that Paul warned Timothy would come. *But realize this, that in the last days difficult times will come... people will hold ... to a form of godliness, although they have denied its power; Avoid such men as these* (2 Tim 3:1, 5). To participate in the great awakening that is stirring in the earth, we need to repent of neglecting such a crucial part of our message and return to the Gospel of power that Jesus preached and demonstrated.

GOSPEL MISSION

Jesus came to destroy the works of the devil (1 John 3:8). He did not protest the injustices of His day but rather introduced the reign of heaven. He addressed sickness and the demonic with the culture of heaven. By the power of the Holy Spirit, He healed the sick, He raised the dead and He delivered people from the demonic. With each release of His power, the kingdom of God advanced in the earth and the kingdom of darkness was driven back.

He did confront the religious culture of His day because they stood in the way of people receiving the new life He was offering. He healed on the Sabbath because the culture of heaven was counter to the religious culture that held people in bondage. The religious laws put in place to preserve the past now hindered the way forward.

When the disciples looked back on the life of Jesus, they reminded people of His mission. *You know of Jesus of Nazareth, how God anointed Him with the Holy Spirit and with power, and how He went about doing good and healing all who were oppressed by the devil, for God was with Him* (Acts 10:38). The anointing of the Holy Spirit resulted in healing being released through His ministry. His life embodied the goodness of His Father so the world could see who the Father really was.

We read in the book of Acts that Jesus' ministry was proven, certified, and validated by miracles. *Men of Israel, listen to these words: Jesus the Nazarene, a man attested to you by God with miracles and wonders and signs which God performed through Him in your midst, just as you yourselves know* (Acts 2:22). The word *attested* used here means "witnessed" – literally God testified on Jesus' behalf. God approved of Jesus' message because it represented His nature. Jesus reached out to heal and God confirmed that it was His heart and desire. As He healed people Jesus perfectly represented the Father and the Father confirmed it with signs and wonders.

MARKED BY MIRACLES

From the beginning of time, God's dealing with mankind has been marked by the miraculous. To be in fellowship with God is to learn to live in a culture where miracles are normal. God instituted life as we know it with His creative power, meaning that the whole realm of our existence began with miracles. The natural realm came into being through the Word of God and is sustained by His power. From the beginning of time, miracles defined God's interaction with His people.

Look at the life of Moses, Joshua, Elijah and Elisha and then ask yourself why the Old Covenant was so marked by Divine intervention and yet we do not expect this today in our 'enlightened' culture. Unfortunately, in the religious systems of today, **expectations are too often set by our experience rather than by the truth.** We live in a naturalistic culture where the prevailing worldview sees the natural as more real than the spiritual realm. So our cultural understanding is limited to the natural realm, which then shapes our beliefs and explains our experience.

When we read the Bible with this worldview we interpret it consistent with our experience and this experiential interpretation becomes our doctrine. Instead of pursuing the miracles we make excuses for not experiencing them. We justify our powerlessness because it is easier and less painful than facing it. Today, right now, let us ask the Holy Spirit to open our eyes to a reality we have not seen. Without miracles we have a powerless message, producing a powerless church. If we are to stem the tide of unbelief in our society, miracles must be restored. They were and always will be a central part of the good news and their restoration is essential if we want to see real sustained revival.

At twenty-five Justin (the name is altered) already had a whole string of felonies. Farley, one of the pastors, sat with him in the church office and heard his current need: gas money to get home to see a dying uncle. He listened, tried to encourage him, gave him some gas money and shared the gospel with him, but he showed little interest.

As he was ready to leave, he agreed to let Farley pray for him, so he asked God to touch Justin with a revelation of His great love. When he finished, Justin was rubbing his arms and looking around like he had seen a ghost. Farley asked what had happened, and he said, "I felt a hand holding my arm, like this," indicating by grabbing his left forearm with his other hand. "Then I felt things leaving out of my hand!" (That's one we'd never heard).

Farley then had a word of knowledge that he had been healed of wrist pain, and he told them that he had arthritis in his right hand. Moving his fingers, he was surprised that he had no pain and had full movement in his hand. Farley then asked him if he had back trouble, and he shared that he had scoliosis. With a little encouragement, he tried touching his toes; again, he was surprised at the results, saying, "I haven't been able to do that for years." No one even prayed for these conditions; his healing was a love gift from God.

By this time Justin was smiling, a little shocked that God loved him so much even in all of his brokenness. Before he was skeptical and unsure, but now he was ready. He asked Jesus to be his Lord and Savior; the smile on his face and the new light in his eyes revealed that something powerful had happened. He encountered the goodness of God and found Him irresistible.

WORD AND POWER

The apostle Paul explained the gospel to the Corinthians leaving little doubt that miracles were inherent in the message. *And my message and my preaching were not in persuasive words of wisdom, but in demonstration of the Spirit and of power, so that your faith should not rest on the wisdom of men, but on the power of God* (1 Cor 2:4-5). Rather than fearing that signs and wonders would deceive men and women, Paul wanted their faith to be anchored in both the Word of God and the demonstration of His power.

When the word is preached with expectation, the Spirit demonstrates the validity of the word. We read that, *God was performing extraordinary miracles by the hands of Paul* (Acts 19:11). Why? Because he expected it and believed that when he declared the goodness of God, the Holy Spirit would back him up. In another account, we read ... *that the father of Publius was lying in bed afflicted with recurrent fever and dysentery; and Paul went in to see him and after he had prayed, he laid his hands on him and healed him. After this had happened, the rest of the people on the island who had diseases were coming to him and getting cured* (Acts 28:8, 9).

Did you read the end of that last verse? It says all the sick that came to him received their healing. The anointing that Jesus carried to heal all who came to Him then rested on Paul. This was not reserved only for a special time period. It demonstrated God's desire that we raise the level of our expectation.

The first time I witnessed this was in the prayer line on our first trip to Brazil. Dr. Randy Clark had preached and demonstrated the power of the Spirit and then the team was called forward to pray. After the first person I prayed for received their healing, I was just relieved that I would not be embarrassed. Then when the second, third and fourth person I prayed for was healed, I felt my mind beginning to tilt. That night I prayed for more than 20 people and every one of them received their healing. The experience shifted something. I believed that Jesus could heal and that He wanted to heal, but that night the bar shot to a new level.

About a year later, Sally and I witnessed 'all' for the first time in a meeting in the Philippines. I asked everyone who needed healing to stand and about half of the 400 people stood. I had them pray with one another and when we asked them to check their bodies out, everyone that stood had been healed, including a man in a wheelchair who had suffered a stroke. When I asked everyone to stand, the man took God at His word and stood to his feet and in the act of faith he was healed. I asked several times if there were any who had not been healed, but the leaders of the church confirmed that all had been healed.

We have only experienced this a few times now, but what we have seen has fueled our appetite for more. The same Holy Spirit that rested on Jesus, rested on the apostle Paul and today rests on each believer willing to step out of his or her comfort zone and give Him some "risk," I mean "faith" to work with. The Gospel is only fully presented, preached or fulfilled when it is demonstrated with power (Rom 15:19).

Ask God to begin to demonstrate through you the proving of His nature. He wants to prove Himself to people through us if we would only step out. If we always play it safe, we give the Holy Spirit no opportunity to validate the word of the gospel and people are left to reason out their walk with God. However, if we will introduce them to a gospel of power, they have a much more sure foundation for their faith. The witness of God at work in their life leaves an indelible mark on them forever.

WE SPEAK WHAT WE BELIEVE

It really does matter what we believe. Paul told the church that, *...having the same spirit of faith, according to what is written, 'I believed, therefore I spoke,' we also believe, therefore also we speak* (2 Cor 4:13). We speak what we believe; so to change the outcome we must change the belief. We simply cannot move beyond the core beliefs that we hold. We can only pray with confidence if we believe correctly because any doubt is the enemy of faith. So, what do we believe about healing?

There are three prevalent views of the place of healing in the Gospel. I was raised with the view that healing has passed away. This view comes from the belief that healing was a gift given to the apostles to confirm their authority to write scripture, but that as the church matured most of the gifts including healing and tongues ceased. Fortunately, those who still hold this view have become the minority because most of the church growth in recent years has been among those who still embrace the gifts of the Holy Spirit.

When we graduated out of the first view we embraced the second, which understands healing as a "special grace" given to some. Those who believe this teach that healing only happens as a sovereign act and reject the idea that healing is in the atonement. They believe that God can heal but are unsure when it is His will to heal. This is still the most prevalent view in the protestant church. Those who hold this position believe that if God does not heal a person, then he or she must accept the sickness as the will of God.

The third view is where we live today. We believe that healing is a part of God's redemptive plan and belongs to every believer. Because healing is both in God's nature and was purchased on the cross, we assume it is God's will to heal even when we do not see it manifest. This allows us to pray for the sick with confidence and faith while we leave the results up to God. We believe that healing and miracles are an integral part of the gospel and need to be restored to the body of Christ if we are to see real sustained revival.

It really does matter what we believe. If we do not believe that healing is rooted in God's redemptive plan, it will prove almost impossible to exercise persistent faith. The problem with the "special grace" view is that in Scripture, the emphasis is not on God's sovereignty, but on faith. Again and again, Jesus told those who were healed, "Your faith has healed you." Not once did He imply that it was a result of God's sovereignty. A person can only have sure faith if he or she holds to the view that healing is in God's redemptive plan. Our view determines the faith we exercise when we pray for the sick.

HEALING AND THE ATONEMENT

Some have a fear that if we believe healing is in the atonement and people are not healed, it will cause them to doubt their salvation. We believe this is based on a wrong comparison. It is not valid to equate healing with our forgiveness or our position of righteousness before God. However, it is perfectly valid to equate healing with sanctification – righteousness is purchased for every believer, and yet not all believers appropriate all that is available to them. In the same way, though healing is available as part of our atonement, not everyone will press in to appropriate all that Christ made available to them. Now let's look at the Biblical foundation for this truth.

Early in His ministry Jesus went to the temple and read from the prophet Isaiah. He turned to the prophetic word over His life that would define His life and mission and by implication, ours. *The Spirit of the Lord is upon Me, because He anointed Me to preach the gospel to the poor. He has sent Me to proclaim release to the captives, And recovery of sight to the blind, to set free those who are downtrodden, To proclaim the favorable year of the Lord* (Luke 4:18-19 quoting Isa 61).

The Messiah would declare the favorable year of the Lord. Peter refers back to Isaiah as well when He speaks of Christ's work on the cross, *and He Himself bore our sins in His body on the cross, so that we might die to sin and live to righteousness; for by His wounds you were healed* (1 Pet 2:24). Many still ask if Peter is referring to physical healing or just to spiritual healing. I grew up with a belief that physical healing is not in the atonement. My teachers' fear was that there would be a crisis of faith if we equate physical and spiritual healing too closely.

This is crucially important because if it's only spiritual, then healing is limited. I remember wrestling with this as I came into the baptism in the Spirit. I had been taught that it was only spiritual and accepted this understanding as truth. Then one day I was reading Matthew and it all changed in a moment. *When evening came, they brought to Him many who were demon-possessed; and He cast out the spirits with a word, and healed all who were ill. This was to fulfill what was spoken through Isaiah the prophet: 'He Himself took our infirmities and carried away our diseases'* (Matt 8:16, 17). Suddenly I saw it; Jesus Himself tied physical healing to the Isaiah passage. The healing taking place in the crowd was clearly more than spiritual healing.

Thus, Isaiah's word refers to both spiritual and physical healing, which means that Jesus directly links physical healing to His atoning work. Jesus died for our sicknesses as well as our sins. This means we should have just as much confidence that God will heal our bodies as we have that He will forgive our sins. We must also understand that connection between healing and the atonement proves that it is not God's will for His people to be sick. We must answer the question: Does God want to heal? Our answer is a resounding Yes!

MIRACLES AND THE COMMISSION

The book of Acts begins with a striking statement. *The first account I composed, …about all that Jesus began to do and teach* (Acts 1:1). Acts is a follow on from the book of Luke with the same author writing an account to show the continuity of the message and work of the Gospel. The wording "all that Jesus began to do" would seem to indicate that what Jesus started now continues. This idea is further strengthened by the inclusion in the original text of the Greek particle *eta*[1] which carries the idea of "on the one hand." Thus, what Jesus did is on the one hand and now on the other hand, what the disciples do is a continuation of the life and ministry of Jesus. So, the book of Acts is a book about what the disciples did as a continuation of the life and ministry of Jesus.

This pattern extends to us as believers today. In His final commission to the disciples, he told us to do everything He commanded. *All authority has been given to Me in heaven and on earth. Go therefore and make disciples of all the nations, baptizing them in the name of the Father and the Son and the Holy Spirit, teaching them to observe all that I commanded you; and lo, I am with you always, even to the end of the age* (Matt 28:18-20).

All authority was given to Jesus and He commissions us with the same commission He gave to His disciples. He is expecting us to operate as a continuation of His life and ministry here on earth. In fact, John clearly states that *... as He is, so also are we in this world* (1 John 4:17). Jesus demonstrated the goodness of His Father and then activated His disciples to do the same. He sent them out to do exactly what He did and He sends us to do no less.

We have established a foundation for signs and wonders to be restored to the Gospel. In the next three chapters, we want to look at healing, words of knowledge and prophecy as three of the gifts that need to be taken out of the house and used as a regular part of our lives. The gifts of the Spirit are tools for the harvest and it is time for every believer to learn to use the tools. The gift of healing operates as the hand of God, releasing His power. Words of knowledge help us see what God sees in a situation and opens the door for His power to be released. Finally, the prophetic allows us to speak the things that are on God's heart for the people He loves but who do not yet know Him.

CHAPTER 9

HEAL THE SICK

DEMONSTRATING THE EXTENT OF THIS GREAT SALVATION

In a meeting in Brazil in September 2012, we prayed for a young man named Lucas. He came up to our prayer line in response to a word of knowledge given about blindness. He told us that he had been born blind in his left eye. We laid our hands on his eye and declared sight in Jesus' name, but after praying a couple of times there was no change. We asked a few more questions and found out that he had been born with no connection between the optic nerve and the back of his left eye. We prayed again, commanding the optic nerve to grow in the name of Jesus and declaring a connection between the optic nerve and the eye. When he opened his eye, he could see light for the first time in his life.

We prayed again, speaking life to all the parts of the eye. When he checked it out, he could begin to see features on the faces of those of us standing around him, but not clearly. So we prayed again and spoke to the muscles controlling the lens and this time he found to his delight that he could read the words on the overhead screen. He had received at least 70% of his sight in the eye. Afterward, he told us that he had visited many doctors and all had told him that there was no hope without a miracle. I love creative miracles!

PERSONAL JOURNEY

Sally and I have for a number of years embraced physical healing as a normal part of the life of the church. There have been seasons where we have seen regular significant breakthroughs and other times where it seemed nothing worked. In the mid 80's through the ministry of Ian Andrews, we entered a season where we saw some very significant miracles but through a number of difficulties and disappointments, we backed off. Not a lot, but just enough that we did not have to face the difficult questions we were being asked about why some received their healing while others who appeared more deserving did not.

About the same time as the outpouring at Toronto we again began to see a resurgence of healing. For the next few years as we planted the church in Springfield, Missouri, we saw fairly regular breakthroughs, just enough to keep us encouraged. Then a few years ago we began to feel the stirring for more and I ran across this prophecy given to Lester Sumrall in 1939 by Smith Wigglesworth. It confirmed the things we were feeling and seeing about the coming awakening.

> "I see the greatest revival in all of the history of mankind coming to planet earth, maybe as never before. And I see the dead raised. I see every form of disease healed. I see whole hospitals being emptied with no one there. Even the doctors are running down the streets shouting." He went on to tell Lester of the multitudes that would be saved in this tremendous worldwide outpouring of the Spirit. "Because nobody will be able to count those who come to Jesus. No disease will be able to stand before God's people."[1]

One morning as we began to press in to see more healing, I heard the Lord ask me a question, "Are you going to back off this time?" I knew exactly what He was asking and made the commitment without hesitation that we would not back off. Shortly after this the Lord divinely connected us with Dr. Randy Clark and Global Awakening. The impartation we received through this relationship and ministering with him in Brazil has catapulted us into experiencing the kinds of signs and wonders we have dreamed of for years.

In the previous chapter, we laid the foundation for healing being included in the atonement and present today as a continuation of the ministry of Jesus. In this chapter, we will lay out four more biblical foundations for the presence of healing in the church today. These are healing as a gift of the Holy Spirit, healing as an expression of the Father's nature, healing as an expression of the goodness of God, and finally, healing as a manifestation of the kingdom.

HEALING AS A GIFT OF THE HOLY SPIRIT

Scripture connects the healing ministry of Jesus directly to the power of the Holy Spirit. We see this when Luke wrote Peter's summary of Jesus' ministry. *You know of Jesus of Nazareth, how God anointed Him with the Holy Spirit and with power, and how He went about doing good and healing all who were oppressed by the devil, for God was with Him* (Act 10:38). Jesus operated in and through the power of the Spirit when He did His mighty works. Jesus confirmed this when He said, *"But if I by the Spirit of God cast out demons, then is the kingdom of God come upon you"* (Matt 12:28 ASV). Look at the wording, "If I by the Spirit." Jesus acknowledged that He did miraculous things by the power of the Spirit. He showed us what a person can do who is full of the Holy Spirit.

Jesus set the standard and then passed that power on to the disciples. The power He gave them came from the Holy Spirit, giving them the ability to do the works that He did. In this, He established a pattern of continuity. Jesus did it, He sent the 12 to do it and then He sent seventy more to do it (Lk. 10:1). When the last group returned after their adventure, they appeared overwhelmed with the power and authority they had walked in. We can hear it in their voices when they say, *...Lord, even the demons are subject to us in Your name* (Luke 10:17). Each one had been sent out with the power of attorney to use the name of Jesus. They had witnessed an authority in Jesus that they had now been given. And the glory of this is that it extends to today as He sends each of us to do it.

Toward the end of His ministry, Jesus knew that it was time for them to live in all that they had experienced by impartation. He called them together and said, *"And behold, I am sending forth the promise of My Father upon you; but you are to stay in the city until you are clothed with power from on high"* (Luke

24:49). Basically, Jesus is saying, "You have been with Me, you have seen Me do it, you have even participated with Me. But now you need more if you are going to complete the task I'm leaving for you."

In Acts we read of their encounter with the Holy Spirit. It started with a promise. *But you shall receive power when the Holy Spirit has come upon you; and you shall be My witnesses both in Jerusalem, and in all Judea and Samaria, and even to the remotest part of the earth* (Acts 1:8). The mark of the Spirit coming on them was **power**. The power of the Holy Spirit gave them a boldness to witness, but it was more than words. They were empowered to do the works of Jesus.

If Jesus did what He did as a man full of the Holy Spirit, then when we live full of the Holy Spirit, we should expect to see the same kinds of things that Jesus saw. The Holy Spirit manifests through us with His gifts, the same gifts that Jesus exercised while He was here on earth. For this chapter, we focus on the gift of healing. Paul's teaching on the gifts included, *...and to another gifts of healing by the same Spirit* (1 Cor 12:9 KJV). Thus, gifts of healing are made available by the Spirit's power. If we need healing for a situation, the Spirit makes it available. Notice that the word "gift" is plural. We see the gift as the healing a person receives, rather than as a reference to a gifted person. Meaning that healing is available without limits.

But for healing to flow as God intends, we need to exercise our faith in order to give the Holy Spirit the opportunity to work. If we always play it safe, we give the Holy Spirit little opportunity to validate the word. This could explain why healing still seems so scarce. Luke assures us, however, that if we will press in, we will find the Holy Spirit just as active as He was with the apostles. *For the promise is for you and your children, and for all who are far off, as many as the Lord our God will call to Himself* (Acts 2:39). The promise is that the Holy Spirit will use us in healing and miracles. The promise is that if we will believe Him, He will empower us to do what Jesus did. The promise is that as we move into awakening, we will see the promise fulfilled.

One evening in Brazil, I prayed with a man who had a degenerative disease that had weakened his whole body and severely affected his balance. He had not walked in 5 years and after a year of physical therapy was told that he would never walk again. As we prayed for him all the pain left his legs and he found he could stand up. After some prayer for his balance, he was able to walk unassisted. The goodness of God is indescribable!

In the same meeting, Sally prayed with a woman who came forward with considerable swelling in her abdominal area. Earlier in the service, she had responded to a word of knowledge and had been healed of a skin condition. Now she told us she had tumors in her abdominal area. Sally prayed for the tumors to dry up and for her body to function properly. She fell under the power of the Spirit, and when she got up after several minutes, she realized that her stomach had shrunk to half its previous size. She was elated!!

HEALING IS IN THE FATHER'S NATURE

Not only is healing a gift of the Spirit, it is a manifestation of the Father's nature. The Spirit does not make it up on His own, but rather He sees what the Father is doing and acts to see it manifest on the earth. One of the names of God is Healer (Exod 15:26). The names of God reveal His character and nature. When He says, *I am the Lord your Healer,* it means that healing is in His nature as a part of who He is. No one begs God to love someone because love is part of His nature. In the same way, we do not have to beg Him to heal. He is willing and eager to bring healing. God is the same today as He was when He revealed His name. He does not change, so we can be confident that He will still reveal Himself as the healer today.

The Gospel of Mark assures us that the power Jesus walked in still functions today. *And these signs will accompany those who have believed: in My name they will drive out demons, they will speak with new tongues… they will place their hands on sick people, and they will get well* (Mark 16:17 NIV). We are promised that signs will follow, so if we believe in His name, we will see healing just as He did. God will prove His word by revealing His goodness and healing people. We are told that *…they went out and preached everywhere, while the Lord worked with them, and confirmed the word by the signs (attesting miracles) that followed* (Mark 16:20). The Lord worked with them. They spoke the Word and God demonstrated His nature, and with every miracle, He proved the validity of His word.

In September 2012, we prayed for a woman with a genetic condition that caused deterioration in the retina. Both her mother and grandmother had gone blind and she was rapidly losing her vision. She had undergone some corrective surgery in the right eye to slow the deterioration and she was scheduled to go in for the same surgery on her left eye. We prayed several times and each time we saw some improvement but then progress stopped with only about 50% of her vision restored. We were a little disappointed that we did not see more improvement, but we encouraged her that God was working and to continue to believe for full restoration even while she slept.

Two nights later she came back to the meeting having been to see her eye doctor. After examining her eyes, he said that he could not explain what he had found. Each eye had a completely new retina with no evidence of disease, and she now had perfect vision! He could not even find evidence of scaring from the surgery that he had performed. Hallelujah, that is the goodness of God revealed!

HEALING AND THE GOODNESS OF GOD

We believe that God is always good, which means that it is His will to heal even if we have not learned to access it. The good news is that healing is more about God's goodness and grace than it is about our performance. David had a real revelation when he wrote, *Taste and see that the Lord is good* (Ps 34:8 NLT). The deeper we go in relationship to our heavenly Father the more we agree with David's assessment. We serve a God who pardons our sins and heals our diseases (Ps 103:3).

In the process of leading the children of Israel out of Egypt and into the Promised Land, Moses faced a whole host of challenges. But he soon realized that God always came through and the revelation led him to a bold request, *I pray Thee, show me Thy glory!* (Exod 33:18). This request came after the burning bush, after the plagues in Egypt, after crossing the Red Sea, after the pillar of cloud by day and fire by night and after the cloud, thunder and lightning descending on the mountain. Moses had seen so much, but the more he saw the more he wanted.

God's answer provided the more that Moses wanted and the more that the body of Christ needs today. *"I Myself will make all My goodness pass before you, and will proclaim the name of the Lord before you; and I will be gracious to whom I will be gracious, and will show compassion on whom I will show compassion"* (Exod 33:19). God answered the request to see His glory with a revelation of all His goodness. In revealing His goodness He established a new facet of His nature. He is glorious and His glory manifests as goodness. His goodness is His glory! This is why one of the fruit of the Spirit is goodness (Gal 5:22). The fruit of the Spirit are character traits of God fleshed out in Jesus and worked into us by the Holy Spirit.

Most of us spend our entire lives trying to please God, but a revelation of the goodness of God will draw us into deeper fellowship with Him. This revelation of the goodness of God powers the awakening. As the true extent of God's goodness manifests, it reveals His grace and compassion, which changes hearts and minds. A true revelation of the goodness of God leads us to repentance (Rom 2:4). It is the goodness of God that made a way for our salvation. It is the goodness of God that heals our bodies, minds and emotions. The goodness of God put His Spirit on us to release His goodness to others, and it is the goodness of God that compels us to go out and touch others.

A few years ago we had a man leave our church angry. He was mad at God and mad at the church. Farley, one of our pastors, visited him in a motel room and found him half drunk and in a foul mood. As soon as he saw Farley he began cursing God and cursing the church, blaming both for all his troubles. Farley knew there was nothing much he could say to change his mind, but after he had quieted down a little bit, Farley asked if he would allow him to pray for him. The man had lost his job in part because of an injury to his rotator cuff, which had been torn in three places (the injury that helped convince him that God was against him). The moment Farley prayed, God healed his shoulder.

When Farley left the room a little while later he was in tears and remembers saying to God, "I do not think I know You very well - a man cusses at You, and You respond by healing him." We've come to know the goodness of God better since then, but the grace He showed the man was a liberating revelation. A few weeks later the guy showed up again at Dayspring Church with a big smile on his face. God's grace really has transforming power.

HEALING AND THE KINGDOM

John the Baptist announced the impending arrival of the kingdom when he preached, *"Repent for the kingdom of heaven is at hand"* (Matt 3:2). He expected a new king, with David as his example. He imagined the Messiah overcoming all their enemies and bringing peace. He introduced Jesus as the one and watched His popularity rise. John had correctly stepped into the background, waiting for the kingdom, but things were not going quite as he had expected.

John had been following the works of Jesus (Matt 11:2), but he saw a problem. Jesus did not fit his concept of the Messiah. And then, waiting in prison about to die unjustly, it looked like Jesus was doing nothing about it. In his confusion, John struggled with unmet expectations and sent his disciples to ask the question, *"Are you the expected one?"* Jesus, clearly aware of his struggle, sent the disciples back with a more accurate view of the kingdom. *Go and report to John what you hear and see; the blind receive sight and the lame walk, the lepers are cleansed and the deaf hear, and the dead are raised and the poor have the good news preached* (Matt 11:4, 5).

Jesus saw the kingdom from a power demonstration point of view. A few verses later He said, *"From the days of John the Baptist until now the kingdom of heaven suffers violence and violent men take it by force"* (Matt 11:12). Jesus' kingdom is doing violence against darkness by signs and wonders, which means for us today that every time someone gets healed the Kingdom of God advances.

However, when it does not happen like we hoped, we open ourselves to being offended. Jesus refers to John's disappointment when he says, *"And blessed is he who does not take offense at Me"* (Matt 11:6). We can easily get offended when God apparently does not come through like we had hoped or when our expectations are not met. A short study of the word "offended" will reveal that one of the meanings is to scandalize, even to the point where we fall away from faith. Literally, getting offended opens us to unbelief that entices us to sin.

PROCLAIMING AND PERFORMING

Everywhere Jesus went He spoke about His Father and about the kingdom. But He did not just talk about it. He demonstrated its reality. *And Jesus was going about in all Galilee, teaching in their synagogues, and proclaiming the gospel of the kingdom, and healing every kind of disease and every kind of sickness among the people* (Matt 4:23). God always intended that He would attest the gospel of the kingdom by demonstrating it with healing so that it moves beyond just a rational message and becomes a revelation message.

Once Jesus had demonstrated this pattern of kingdom expansion, He sent His disciples out to *proclaim the kingdom of God, and to perform healing* (Luke 9:2). The same things happened when they did what they had seen Jesus do. When they proclaimed the Kingdom, the rule of heaven touched earth and released the works of the Kingdom. When the rule of God invades this age, something will happen. In the next chapter of Luke, we read that He did it again but this time with seventy (Luke 10:9), with similar results.

Paul brings this forward to the church today when he wrote, *for the kingdom of God does not consist in words, but in power* (1 Cor 4:20). Today God is still in the same business, demonstrating His rule with Word and power, and He has equipped us by His Spirit to go throughout the earth doing what Jesus did.

We know from church history that miracles continued in the church even though they were not as widespread as they should have been. There are several mentions of this in the writings of early theologians, but I like what Novatian, one of the church fathers, had to say. Somewhere around A.D. 270, he wrote a treatise, which gave an impassioned defense of the trinity. In the section on the Holy Spirit, he spoke of the key role the Spirit played in empowering the church. Here is my favorite passage.

They were henceforth armed and strengthened by the same Spirit, having in themselves the gifts which this same Spirit distributes, and appropriates to the Church, the spouse of Christ, as her ornaments. This is He who places prophets in the Church, instructs teachers, directs tongues, gives powers and healings, does wonderful works, often discrimination of spirits, affords powers of government, suggests counsels, and orders and arranges whatever other gifts there are of charismata; and thus make the Lord's Church everywhere, and in all, perfected and completed.[2]

This is as true today as it was then. Novatian died a martyr during the persecution of Christians by the Roman emperor. But his writings make it clear that a few years before the conversion of Constantine, the gifts of the Spirit including healing were still in operation and vital to perfecting and completing the church.

The mandate of Jesus is the mandate for today. John wrote, *for this purpose the Son of God was manifested, that he might destroy the works of the devil* (1 John 3:8 KJV). The job or assignment of destroying the works of the devil initiated through Christ now happens through us. We have the privilege and the responsibility of doing the works of Jesus today as a continuance of His ministry.

CHAPTER 10

SUPERNATURAL INSIGHT

ACCESSING INFORMATION NEEDED FOR BREAKTHROUGH

One of the most dramatic healings through a Word of Knowledge we have ever witnessed happened a couple of years ago in a meeting in Brazil. The presence of God was awesome in worship and Dr. Randy Clark had great liberty as he preached with many receiving their healing as he shared some powerful testimonies. When he had finished, he called the team to give words of knowledge. Early on someone gave a word about a deaf right ear. The moment the word was given, a girl in the back of the room who was deaf from birth began to pat her hand against her right ear and it popped open.

Then a few minutes later another person gave a word of knowledge for a deaf left ear. The same girl began to pat her left ear and it opened. Remember, although she could now hear with her right ear she still has no comprehension of language in order to understand the second word. It was a miracle on so many levels. The only way we knew what had happened was that her father brought her forward and gave the testimony. From his vantage point, sitting right beside her, he witnessed his daughter's reaction to the words and confirmed that she started out totally deaf and unable to hear the word given. Absolutely stunning! The word of knowledge itself carried the power to manifest the healing to ears that could not hear.

Reinhard Bonnke had an encounter with God that forever changed his perspective. He had been asking for greater breakthrough, when one night he heard the Spirit say something that was life changing "My word in your mouth is as powerful as My word in My mouth."[1]

THE POWER OF HIS WORD

The story of creation gives ample evidence of the power of God's spoken word. *Then God said, "Let there be light;" and there was light* (Gen 1:3). Disorder and chaos ruled the earth until the Spirit of God spoke, bringing order to chaos. We find a principle here. When God wants to bring order He sends His Spirit and He speaks a word. When we do His work, we should expect to operate in the power of His Spirit, and we should expect to speak His word to bring healing, deliverance and salvation.

We see this principle in action in God's revelation of Himself as healer. God's promise to His people was that, *...If you will give earnest heed to the voice of the Lord your God, and do what is right in His sight, and give ear to His commandments, and keep all His statutes, I will put none of the diseases on you which I have put on the Egyptians; for I, the Lord, am your healer* (Exod 15:26). The name used here, Jehovah Rapha, means the God who heals, mends, cures, repairs and makes thoroughly whole. The name reveals the character and nature of the God they are getting to know, so with this new name the people understand that healing is in the very nature of God.

The context of the revelation of His name as healer is intriguing. Three days after His people cross the Red Sea, they come to an oasis called Marah where they found the water undrinkable. The people have quickly forgotten the powerful hand of God displayed in the deliverance from the Egyptian army and they began to grumble to Moses.

Moses' admirable response is to turn to God for a solution. *Then he cried out to the Lord, and the Lord showed him a tree; and he threw it into the waters, and the waters became sweet...* (Exod 15:25). The Lord showed him a tree. The word translated *tree* in this verse is a general word for a tree but it could just as well be used for a stick or "a piece of wood."[2] So the Lord's instruction was to throw that piece of wood into the water. God gave Moses a word of knowledge – throw a particular chunk of wood into the pond – and when Moses obeyed, the water was healed.

God chose to use a word of knowledge in the act of revealing Himself as the healer. This means that God established a direct connection between the word of knowledge and healing. So the gift of Word of knowledge is a gift that we should expect to be closely connected with healing. Back to our starting principle - when God wants to heal, He speaks the word to unlock the faith needed for the miracle. All that we add is obedience - taking the risk to speak what we hear and do what needs to be done. The word of knowledge is like a stick thrown into the bitter waters. Catch the stick and you get the healing.

David must have understood this when he wrote, *He sent His word and healed them...* (Ps 107:20). He knew the power of the word of God and knew that a Word from God could release healing. The word of knowledge carries with it the healing power of God. This is why we often see people healed after words of knowledge are given, even before we pray. If it really is a word from God, we should not be surprised if the word itself releases healing.

WORD OF KNOWLEDGE

When we go to the New Testament, Paul gives us the vocabulary for the principle we saw in shadow. *But to each one is given the manifestation of the Spirit for the common good. For to one is given the word of wisdom through the Spirit, and to another the word of knowledge according to the same Spirit* (1 Cor 12:7-8). If we have received the empowering of the Holy Spirit, the gifts are immediately available for our use. Notice that the gifts serve the common good – they are given to us to meet the needs of those we minister to. The gifts of the Holy Spirit were never intended to be seen as merit badges of achievement, but rather as tools for ministry to others. I like the way Bill Johnson puts it. "The Holy Spirit is in you for you but on you for others."

Does this make the gift of word of knowledge available to anyone who needs it? For the answer let's look at some of what Paul says about the gifts in general. *Now I wish that you all spoke in tongues, but even more that you would prophesy; and greater is one who prophesies than one who speaks in tongues, unless he interprets, so that the church may receive edifying* (1 Cor 14:5). Paul's statement here is an encouragement for all believers to speak in tongues and prophesy. By implication this makes the gifts available to all. It is not wrong to assume that all can operate in the word of knowledge. In fact, we see the gifts as tools in a toolbox waiting for us to use them.

The gifts are manifestations of the Spirit. The word manifestation simply means that the invisible becomes visible. Or that which has not been experienced can now be experienced. The Holy Spirit is at work to bring the invisible God into visible action in the earth. *But one and the same Spirit works all these things, distributing to each one individually just as He wills* (1 Cor 12:11). It would appear then that the gifts, distributed by the will of the Spirit, are made available based on the need of the moment.

Earlier in the same letter, Paul affirms this work of the Spirit to bring revelation by the manifestations of the Spirit. *Now we have received, not the spirit of the world, but the Spirit who is from God, that we might know the things freely given to us by God, which things we also speak, not in words taught by human wisdom, but in those taught by the Spirit, combining spiritual thoughts with spiritual words* (1 Cor 2:12-13). The word of knowledge comes as information from the Spirit, given as a key to unlock the situation – just use it. It is like the stick thrown into the water that brought healing.

When explaining the gift of prophecy Paul made a statement that also would apply to a word of knowledge. *For we know in part and we prophesy in part* (1 Cor 13:9). Just as prophecy is in part, so is the word of knowledge. The word of knowledge comes as a fragment of information from the Spirit. Even though it provides only a small part of the whole picture, it gives the missing piece (or key) to unlock the situation we are facing. God is all-knowing but he only gives us what we need to know at any given moment.

Words of knowledge help us to know and understand situations, circumstances, strategies of the enemy (kingdoms of darkness), etc. It enables us to know how to speak into situations with specific knowledge that can bring answers, understanding, healing and deliverance. **The word of knowledge does not come from any natural source. It is a fragment of supernatural information that comes directly from the Holy Spirit, given for a distinct purpose.**

The word of knowledge releases a supernatural revelation of facts which comes from the mind of God to deal with the present situation. While the gift of prophecy generally speaks from the present to the future, a Word of Knowledge concerns the present or the past. It releases knowledge or information that could not come from human understanding or wisdom.

Although the term "word of knowledge" is not often used in scripture, we can see this operation of the Spirit in both the Old and New Testaments. Elijah is told to go meet Ahab in Naboth's vineyard (1 Kgs 21:18). Elijah has a prophetic word for the king but he needed to know where to find him. The Holy Spirit is well able to give him the king's current location.

Coming over into the New Testament, we read in the book of Acts that Peter heard by the Spirit that three men were looking for him (Acts 10:19). This gives him the right disposition to respond to the servants who will ask him to go minister to the Gentiles. In both of these accounts, the word of knowledge came as a revelation to provide the amount of information necessary for the need of the moment.

EXAMPLES OF A WORD OF KNOWLEDGE FROM SCRIPTURE

- To warn a king of an enemy's plan of destruction (2 Kgs 6:9-12).
- To encourage a discouraged servant of the Lord (1 Kgs 19:14-18).
- To expose a hypocrite (2 Kgs 5:20-27).
- To convince a sinner of the need of a Saviour (John 4:18,19,29).
- To discover a man in hiding (1 Sam 10:22).
- To indicate a man in need (Acts 9:11).
- To reveal corruption in the Church (Acts 5:3).
- To indicate a suitable place for a meeting of God's people (Mark 14: 13-15).
- To know men's thoughts (John 2:24; 1 Sam 9:19).

RECEIVING A WORD OF KNOWLEDGE

Words of knowledge can assist us in many different situations. Anytime people need an encounter with God, He may use a word of knowledge to open the door for their breakthrough. The main advice we would give anyone who desires to operate in this gift is simply to be aware, to quiet your thoughts and look, listen and feel in order to sense how the Holy Spirit might be speaking or directing you. Many times we believe God has things for us to hear but we are just too busy to listen. Different ones of us hear in unique ways. We have listed the ways we have experienced getting words, but the Spirit is not limited and can communicate through any of our senses.

THINK THE WORD

A word of knowledge can come as an impression; it may be the name of an illness or a situation. Often it is only a slight impression so that it takes faith to speak it out. This is the way I most often receive a word. It comes as a fleeting thought or impression that would be easy to ignore, except that I have learned to trust my spiritual intuition. It is difficult to explain because it roots in the spirit, which then manifests in the mind as a thought. Even though we cannot necessarily explain how we received it, we know the thought came at the appropriate moment and with experience have learned to trust what we are hearing.

In an activation session in Florida we had everyone ask for a word of knowledge, then write the first thing that came to his or her mind. A pastor on the front row heard the word "eggs." He was sure he was wrong, but when I asked if it meant something to anyone, the guy sitting right behind him responded. He was the cook who had prepared the pastors' breakfast for us the day before. Somehow he had misplaced several dozen eggs and had been looking for them just before the service. When we prayed for him he remembered a place he had not looked and went to get them.

FEEL THE WORD

One of the common ways a person can receive a word of knowledge comes through feeling the person's pain as a physical symptom. This can manifest as a pain or just an unusual sensation in our body. It can also be an emotion such as fear or panic. This most often comes in association with the gift of healing. Although I seldom experience a word coming in this way, one of our intercessors at Dayspring Church often experiences words for us while we are traveling. If she feels a pain or symptom while she intercedes for us, she will send us a text. More than once I have been in a situation where I needed a word and I would receive a text from her just at the right moment.

Sometimes a word of knowledge is received as an empathetic feeling. It can come as an overwhelming feeling unrelated to our circumstances. This often happens in a ministry situation, when praying with someone. If suddenly we feel an emotion like sadness, or heaviness, or even joy, pay attention to that feeling. It could be a word of knowledge as the Lord allows us to feel something of what the other person is experiencing.

SEE THE WORD

For those who are visual, the word can come as a mental picture. This kind of word can come as a picture. It could be a body part, a person, sometimes even a name of a person. It can also come as a picture of an object or situation. Even if we do not understand what we are seeing, simply give what you see without trying to interpret it. Then the one leading the meeting may ask if it means anything to someone. When we add in details or our own interpretation, we can cause the word to miss the person that God wants to highlight. Some have seen a word written on or over an individual or situation. Others have seen a name or a condition superimposed on people. Some would call this a vision or a visual impression.

A woman on the team during a Brazil trip gave a word she saw as a picture. What she saw was a banana hanging from a string in the living room. I must admit I wondered about it, but a woman in the back of the room responded. Her daughter had suffered from severe migraine headaches so the woman had taken her to the medicine man for healing. She had been told to go home and tie a string to a banana and hang it from the ceiling; it had not helped and in fact, her daughter had gotten worse. But that night the word of knowledge broke the power of witchcraft and the girl was delivered and healed. Then both the mother and daughter got saved. The word of knowledge provided the key to unlocking the family from their history and drew them to repentance.

SAY THE WORD

How many times have we said things without thinking? Well sometimes it is more than just motor mouth; sometimes the Spirit overrides our mind and we find ourselves saying something that had no forethought. This happens frequently when we are counseling and say something we had not thought of before. This kind of word of knowledge overrides our hesitancy in order to unlock a difficult situation. A friend of mine was praying for a young woman who needed a touch from God and they were not getting the breakthrough. After a little while, he stopped praying and began to ask some more questions. In the middle of it, he heard himself say, "When did you have the abortion?" Needless to say, he would have found a more tactful way to approach the subject, but it created the breakthrough that she needed and the woman found freedom and forgiveness.

We have even experienced it with modern technology. During worship in South Dakota, I typed a list of words of knowledge into my phone to use while speaking. When it came time to give the words, I began to read my list. The first two were ok but the third one was not what I had written. I had written, "left side pain" and on my phone, it said "Lacy side pain." I stared at it for a few moments and was not sure what to do. I knew there was a Lacy in the service and knew I would not have written her name knowing she was there. So I told people what had happened and to all of our delight Lacy, in fact, did have left side pain and God healed her. I have tried every combination of misspelling 'left' that I can think of to make autocorrect change it to Lacy and it is still a mystery.

DREAM THE WORD

Dreams frequently have spiritual implications. If it gives revelation into a situation we are facing, it could serve as a word of knowledge. There are several examples in the Old Testament of dreams containing information that someone needed. Some of these were prophetic while others contained a piece of information necessary for the completion of a God-given task. As we come over into the Gospels we see dreams as no less important. Joseph was warned to flee to Egypt and Peter received a revelation of the scope of the gospel.

Our most notable experience with this happened early in our time on the mission field. One night Sally woke having dreamed about Stuart Briscoe, the pastor of a church that supported us. She prayed at length about him and his family. Finally, after several hours the burden lifted, and she went back to sleep. But in the morning, she was intrigued enough that she sat down and wrote a letter to the Briscoe's giving the date and times that she felt to pray and asking if it had any significance.

By the time the letter made it from Kenya to the states, it was many weeks before we got a reply back from the Briscoes. To our delight, at the very moment when the dream woke Sally and she began to pray, Stewart and his daughter were on a mission trip in South America and the daughter suddenly became very ill. The situation was critical, and they had difficulty getting her transported to a hospital. Finally, a small plane got to her and flew her to a hospital. The times matched exactly across the time zones of the earth and the burden to pray did not lift until the daughter had reached safety.

CONTEXT FOR WORDS OF KNOWLEDGE

We have already established that there is a strong connection between words of knowledge and physical healing, but there are contexts other than meetings where they can be used to bring a breakthrough. We see words of knowledge used as a means of bringing people into an encounter with the goodness of God. The world needs to know the love God has for them and the word of knowledge allows us to see what God is seeing in a person. When we give them the word God has given for them, their hearts are opened by His love to a reality they may never have experienced.

OBSERVATIONS FROM EXPERIENCE

It is not unusual for the word we get to be for someone near us in the market-place or in a worship service. God is tuning our spiritual senses to the needs of people around us. He is highlighting them so we can easily respond and pray for them. But having said that, distance makes no difference to God. Also, we should not be surprised if we get more than one word for a person or if several of the words we give end up being for the same person in a meeting. Sometimes God just highlights an individual. I have seen as many as five of the words I gave apply to one individual.

Do not try to interpret the word. Just give it exactly as you heard it and trust the Holy Spirit. I often ask the question "Does this make sense to anyone?" The Holy Spirit is able to take the fragment of information we give and use it to bring a breakthrough. It is essential that we learn to trust what we hear without over thinking it. Children are often better at getting words than adults because they simply trust what they hear. We need to become as children that trust our Father to give us what we need to minister to His people. Your age, education, nationality make no difference.

When we get the word of knowledge, ask more questions of the Holy Spirit. If we heard "knee" ask; Is it the right or the left? Is it a male or a female? Is it from an injury? The more specific we can get, the greater the faith that is released. Ask for more but don't add to what we hear. If we add, we are bringing in our own thinking, and it will cause confusion. A simple word is all God needs to bring a breakthrough in someone's life.

Finally, don't be afraid to practice. If we ask someone if they have a bad elbow and they don't, nothing is lost. Inherent in the grace of God is the right to try and fail and still keep trying. Do not let the enemy put a guilt trip on us, just get up and try again.

CHAPTER 11

PROPHETIC LIFESTYLE

COMMUNICATING GOD'S HEART FOR PEOPLE

We often express our worship at Dayspring Church with prophetic art. One Sunday morning during the service Linda noticed the prophetic artists down front and marveled at how God moved uniquely through each of them. Then one of the paintings caught her eye. Jerry, one of the artists, had started with a black background and then painted a large lightning bolt originating from the top of the picture. The next time she looked, he had painted a large boulder. It appeared that the lightning bolt had struck it and split it in two.

As the service ended Linda walked up to take a closer look at the painting and to read the prophetic word he had written to go with the picture. She first noticed that Jerry had painted the name Barbara at the top of the picture. Then she read the prophetic word that went with it, "You have been going through many trials, but just as this lightening strikes this boulder and removes it, so will I remove the obstacle in your life." Linda knew the instant she read the word that it was meant for her Aunt Barb and shared it with Jerry. Her aunt had been fighting cancer in her mouth, so after checking that there was no one else at the meeting named Barbara, Linda took the painting to give to her aunt.

Her aunt was scheduled for surgery the next week to remove part of her jaw in hopes that would stop the spread of the cancer. The next day, Linda and her husband drove to Kansas City to give her the picture and the prophetic word. Her aunt was amazed and touched at how the Lord knew her by name, knew her situation and cared so much for her. They prayed with her aunt and uncle and could feel hope arise within them. When the doctors went in to perform the surgery later that week, they did not remove the bone, because they could no longer find any cancer! God is so amazing!

ALL GOD'S PEOPLE SHOULD PROPHECY

As the people of God traveled through the wilderness, God showed Moses that he needed to appoint elders to assist him in doing the work. In obedience, Moses called seventy leaders to gather at the tent of meeting. It would appear that sixty-eight showed up, and God took the Spirit that rested on Moses and put it on each of the elders. When the Spirit of God touched them, they each began to prophesy.

Two men, who were apparently invited, had not appeared at the tent for the time of impartation, but they got it anyway. When the Spirit of God touched the group, He also touched the two and they began to prophesy in the camp. When Moses was informed that others prophesied, rather than being concerned, or setting a limit on the use of the gift, Moses' response typifies that of a mature leader. He told Joshua ...Would that all the Lord's people were prophets, that the Lord would put His Spirit on them (Num 11:29). I wish they all could prophesy! Rather than treating prophecy as something for the elite, he expressed the heart of God who wants every believer to hear the voice of the Holy Spirit and then share with others what they heard.

This same sentiment is echoed in the New Testament when Paul tells the Corinthian church, Now I wish that you all spoke in tongues, but even more that you would prophesy (1 Cor 14:5). Paul expresses his desire that every believer would exercise the gift of tongues because the gift edifies the individual. However, he goes on to express an even more pressing desire, for every believer to hear the voice of God and speak it out prophetically.

Speaking in tongues edifies us personally, but when we prophesy the people around us receive the edification. The primary meaning of the word edify is "to build;" so the purpose of the gifts of the Holy Spirit is to build. Regular use of the gift of tongues builds the individual believer in their faith and in their ability to hear the voice of God. While the prophetic, when correctly understood, has a primary purpose of building up and strengthening those around us.

Kenny visited a local school and just as he arrived two teachers were walking into the office. Kenny shared a picture that God had given him for one of them and she began to cry. He then asked her if she had pain in her back. She did, so they prayed for her and the pain left. They all started clapping, which caught the attention of the rest of the office staff, and they came in to see what was going on. When the lady shared that God had healed her back, one of the other staff said she had pain in her back as well. Kenny encouraged the woman who had just been healed to lay hands on the staff member. When she did, God healed her.

Then another teacher was asked if he would like to receive prayer. He said he never had anyone pray for him, but he was open to it. As Kenny prayed for him, he began to prophesy about how God saw him as a knight in shining armor, and he called out the nobility in him. Tears welled up in his eyes. Kenny then asked him if he had back pain, and the young teacher said "Always!" Ever since his time in the military he had suffered a tremendous amount of pain and as a consequence, he had not been able to feel his feet for several years. Everyone in the room laid hands on him and prayed. After the prayer, he said he could feel a tingling in his feet. It surprised him so much that he fell to the floor and began to cry. After a little while, he got up, took off his shoes and said, "I cannot believe I have the feeling back in my feet." They all cheered and reminded him how much God loves us! School is always more fun when God shows up.

RESTORING THE PROPHETIC

The only gift that appears each time Paul lists the gifts and ministries in scripture is "prophecy" or "prophet." Despite this consistency, prophecy and the ministry of the prophet have been neglected and misunderstood. From the time of the reformation, the nature of the prophetic has been under assault. Instead of understanding prophecy as revelation where the prophet speaks under the inspiration of the Holy Spirit, the reformers opted for defining prophecy as interpretation. Prophecy became the prophet's ability to interpret scripture into a present situation. Calvin held this view and wrote in his commentary on 1 Thessalonians.

> By the term prophecy, however, I do not understand the gift of foretelling the future, but as in 1 Corinthians 14:3, the science of interpreting Scripture, so that a prophet is an interpreter of the will of God... Let, therefore, prophecy in this passage be understood as meaning interpretation made suitable to present use.[1]

THIS BASICALLY REDUCES PROPHECY TO PREACHING THE WORD

Much of the Church today has been influenced by this view, understanding the gift of prophesy as forth-telling and associating it with interpreting and speaking out God's Word. It is inevitable that those from the cessationist or dispensational camp would accept this definition but surprisingly, this view extends even into some Pentecostal denominations. While there is no doubt that preaching can and should have a prophetic element, we believe that the revelation or foretelling element Calvin rejects is an essential expression of the prophetic ministry.

Prophecy inspired by the Holy Spirit contains an element of revelation with the responsibility to communicate the mind of God for people's future. The purpose of this kind of prophetic is to produce a hunger in people to pursue God with their whole heart. It would appear that Paul viewed prophecy primarily as revelation when he wrote, *...When you assemble, each one has a psalm, has a teaching, has a revelation, has a tongue, has an interpretation. Let all things be done for edification* (1 Cor 14:26). The word *apokalupsis* meaning "revelation or disclosure" used here, instead of the word *prophetia*, gives us a glimpse into the nature of the prophetic.

This idea of revelation or disclosure provides us with Paul's definition of the word prophetic. Prophecy at its most basic then must be revelation. It cannot simply be wisdom applied to the teaching of the Word. Prophecy must be understood as inspired speech, something that has been spontaneously brought to mind by the Holy Spirit.

This is further reinforced by one of the meanings of the Greek word *pro-feeteia*, "to utter forth, or to declare, a thing that can only be known by divine revelation."[2] From this we would see the gift of prophecy as the special ability that God gives by the Holy Spirit to members of the body to convey God's message for the moment to people. It does not come from a natural skill or ability, but it is the actual speaking forth of revelation given by the Spirit for or in a particular situation.

The Church needs the ministry of the prophet today. Without their foundational work, the Church will never reach its potential (Eph 2:20). The Church also needs the prophetic gifting to be released. Both within the Church and outside in the walls, multitudes wait for the Church to step into her calling and prophesy. For the world to be introduced to their loving Father, we must become the prophetic people we were created to be.

PROCLAIM HIS EXCELLENCIES

Earlier we looked at the truth of the priesthood of the believer, but there is a prophetic function of the believer's priesthood that applies here. Peter wrote, *But you are a chosen race, a royal priesthood, a holy nation, a people for God's own possession, so that you may proclaim the excellencies of Him who has called you out of darkness into His marvelous light* (1 Pet 2:9). As believers, we are the people of God because we have been grafted into an incredible root of promise. That makes us His own special people, His purchased possession. We are a people that have yielded to the Holy Spirit in us, following His lead. When we walk out into the world as His special people, it is easy to be priests, because He who is in us naturally is going to leak out of us. Remember when Isaiah saw the people of God as priests, he also saw them as ministers of God (Isa 61:6).

The revelation of the body as priests also included the action of being ministers. When Peter speaks of proclaiming, he uses a unique word that gives the sense of "publishing abroad." But it means much more than just passing on information. One of the meanings is "to reveal what has been hidden, or to declare what is secret."[3] The word is used in Acts 3:18 and Acts 7:52 to describe the prophetic word of a prophet. The goodness of God has been hidden from the world, but as His priests, we prophetically reveal His goodness to this realm. We are to speak what God is saying to the society around us. The priesthood of the believer requires us to make the prophetic declarations that God wants released through His people. Declarations that will shift the atmosphere, change circumstances and envision people.

Looking deeper into the meaning of the word *proclaim*, we find that it is not just about an idea. It's about an action. The people of God as priests have a dual role. We are to proclaim His glory and demonstrate His goodness. Thus, the prophetic word we speak comes with an accompanying action. Something happens when people are touched by what God is saying. Their hearts and minds are open to Him, and He, through us, demonstrates His love with healing, deliverance and freedom.

PRIESTS REPRESENT JESUS TO THE WORLD

The word *represent* means to present again. As priests, we hear what God is saying and then speak from the unseen realm. We see the works He desires, and then do the works He asks of us - all to represent Jesus to a lost and dying world. Represent means to speak, act, or be present officially for another person or on behalf of them. When we are present for another person, we act as a representative or promoter of their activity. As priests we serve as representatives of Jesus, demonstrating His power, love and grace to the world.

Paul called himself an ambassador - another word for our priestly function. An ambassador is a diplomat sent by a country as its official representative to a foreign country. Priests act as ambassadors of Jesus – present to speak and act on His behalf. They live to proclaim His excellencies thus fulfilling Isaiah's prophecy that *the people whom I formed for Myself will declare My praise* (Isa 43:21).

SIMPLE WORDS WITH PROFOUND EFFECT

In the first chapter, we spoke briefly about the ministry of Gypsy Smith, an evangelist who ministered to millions. We want to come back to him again to tell the story of the prophetic word that sowed the seed of revival into him. He started out in some very humble beginnings and with little hope of a future until God broke into his life with a destiny changing word. In 1874 D. L. Moody, himself a powerful evangelist, visited a gypsy camp in London. At some point, he laid hands on a young boy and said, "May the Lord make a preacher of you, my boy,"[4] just simple words that carried a profound impact. The word penetrated the heart of Gypsy Smith and set him on a course. He bought himself a bible and a dictionary and taught himself to read. Then William Booth gave him an opportunity to preach and the rest is history.

Years later, on Gypsy Smith's first trip to the US, the two men met and Gypsy was able to remind Moody of the prophetic word he had received from him and shared the impact it had on his life. The revival Moody carried awakened a young boy who would follow in his footsteps. We must be careful not to underestimate the power of a simple word released to people in need of hope.

PROPHETIC LIFESTYLE

The goal for every believer should be to live a prophetic lifestyle. This operates not just in meetings but in the whole of our lives. Paul writes, *But if all prophesy, and an unbeliever or an ungifted man enters, he is convicted by all, he is called to account by all; the secrets of his heart are disclosed; and so he will fall on his face and worship God, declaring that God is certainly among you* (1 Cor 14:24-25).

His statement "if all prophesy" proves again that the prophetic gift is available to all. This passage also lays the foundation for our understanding that prophecy can be legitimately used among unbelievers. Prophecy is not just intended for the confines of the building. It can be used to bring conviction to unbelievers who have their hearts ready to hear the word of the Lord.

Some will immediately point to a previous verse that appears to state the opposite, as a caution against prophecy being for unbelievers. While true that 1 Corinthians 14:22 appears to contradict 14:24, we know that Paul was not in the habit of contradicting himself. This means we need to look deeper into the situation he was addressing. Several commentators view the first verse as a rhetorical restatement of an aspect of the local issue he was dealing with, which would make 1 Corinthians 14:24 his response to their justification of using tongues with unbelievers.[5] We believe this is the case, which makes prophecy an essential tool for revealing God's heart to unbelievers. How sad that we have made church meetings the primary context for the exercise of the prophetic, instead of the marketplace.

Leigh uses her prophetic gift regularly in the marketplace. A few months ago she came out of her office one day and noticed one of her students crying on the phone with her fiancé. After she hung up, Leigh asked her what was wrong and how she could help. The student shared with her that she had lost her engagement ring, and her fiancé was furious with her. Leigh told her how God was concerned about this situation in her life. The student kind of rolled her eyes and said they had looked everywhere and could not find it. Then Leigh heard the Lord say, "It's in her car," so she shared what she had heard from God. The student told her she was crazy and said that they had looked there several times. Once again Leigh told her that she knew what God said. He said "It's in your car and to look again." She rolled her eyes and walked away. The next morning Leigh encountered the student again standing just outside her office with a big smile on her face. She held up her hand to show her the ring on her finger. She told Leigh that after she left the school she and her fiancé looked in the car again and found it under the driver seat. They were both amazed. Leigh grabbed her and hugged her and reminded her how much God loves her.

Paul sets the tone for the subject of this chapter when he wrote, *Pursue love, yet desire earnestly spiritual gifts, but especially that you may prophesy* (1 Cor 14:1). Loving our neighbor is a commandment. In the previous chapter, Paul has just laid out his treatise on the priority of love as the motive for all we do. But now he adds something to it. In addition to love, people need to hear the comfort, encouragement and exhortation that only a prophetic word can bring.

As the people of God, we are called to earnestly desire to operate in the gifts of the Holy Spirit. The word Paul uses to describe our desire for spiritual gifts means, to burn with zeal or literally to strive after.[6] We are asked to strive after the blessing of operating in the prophetic. We are to burn with zeal looking for the opportunity to introduce people to our God who loves them and wants to speak to them through us. We must take a risk and step out in faith so that God can use us to demonstrate His love. In fact, love is the main motivation behind the prophetic lifestyle.

PROPHETIC EVANGELISM

Using our prophetic gift in the marketplace becomes prophetic evangelism. The prophetic word has the power to penetrate the defenses people have put up against God. When what we speak cannot be explained naturally, people know it is supernatural. God, who sees the heart of each individual, knows exactly what it will take to open their hearts to hear His voice. Our responsibility is to be led by the Spirit, trusting Him to show us where to go, who to talk to, and what to say. We find it a fascinating side note that it was Philip the evangelist's daughters that were prophetesses (Acts 21:8, 9). Perhaps, in the home of an evangelist, learning to prophesy was normal.

We see prophetic evangelism in operation in the life of Jesus. While traveling through Samaria, He encounters a woman at the well. The prophetic revelation about her love life opened a whole town to the good news (Luke 5:1-11). On another occasion, He spots Zacchaeus up in a tree and prophesies an encounter at his home (Luke 19:1-10). In each case, Jesus by revelation of the Holy Spirit heard what the Father wanted to say and then said it. In the same way, we need to hear from the Holy Spirit what the Father wants us to do or to say, and then release it here on the earth.

Prophetic evangelism goes beyond knowing the facts of the Gospel. If we will listen, the Holy Spirit will give us a word that touches the deepest need of the individual and opens their heart to His love. His word through us lets them know that God is real, that He is for them and that He is good. Using the prophetic in the marketplace is simply about hearing God on their behalf and then sharing it with them.

NATURE OF A PROPHETIC LIFESTYLE

Paul tells us *…everyone who prophesies speaks to men for their strengthening, encouragement and comfort* (1 Cor 14:3). The prophetic gift used in the marketplace falls generally into these three areas. While the word may occasionally be predictive, this would apply more to the ministry of a Prophet than to the operation of the gift of prophecy.

When we exercise the gift of prophecy it brings strength. The purpose is to edify, to build up, and to bring spiritual instruction. The Greek word used here is *oikodome*, which means "the act of building up or promoting another's growth." Prophecy strengthens because it calls out the gold in people. Prophecy promotes another's growth by identifying their destiny and revealing their purpose in God. Prophecy shows them how God sees them and gives them a goal to grow toward.

The gift of prophecy also brings encouragement. The Greek word used here is *paraklesis*, with a direct relationship to the work of the Holy Spirit as our helper. Not surprising that this gift of the Spirit means a calling near, a summons, an entreaty or an admonition. Prophecy encourages people by challenging them to pursue a relationship with God. Prophecy comes alongside a person to exhort them, to advise them, to warn them or to admonish them. Prophecy comes alongside as an invitation to restored intimacy with their Creator.

Finally, the gift of prophecy brings comfort. Its purpose is to bring hope, to bring freedom from worry or pain and to console. The Greek word used here is *paramuthia*, meaning "an address for the purpose of persuading, arousing and stimulating." Prophecy consoles people by persuading them of God's unconditional love. Prophecy brings hope by arousing them out of passivity and stimulating them to action. Prophecy assures people that God is for them even in the midst of difficult circumstances.

DEVELOPING A PROPHETIC LIFESTYLE

The Holy Spirit is calling each of us to make fostering a prophetic lifestyle a personal priority. Developing this lifestyle first requires cultivating a love and compassion for people. Quite simply, we will not take a risk for people we do not love. Love is a commandment and compassion has the power to motivate us to action.

Next, make a commitment to hear on their behalf. This does not mean we passively wait for information but rather calls for actively asking questions of the Holy Spirit. Ask the question, then take the risk and share what we hear with them. Remember, prophecy was never abnormal in scripture, and it needs to become normal for us again.

Finally, developing a prophetic lifestyle means that we must have confidence in our ability to hear the voice of the Holy Spirit. Jesus promised us that His sheep hear His voice (John 10:27). This means that there is no excuse for us not to prophecy. If we can hear Him, we can tell others what we are hearing.

CHAPTER 12

RADIATING HIS GLORY

STEWARDING AND RELEASING THE GLORY OF GOD

One week after Thanksgiving in 2013, Sherri's aunt suddenly experienced a severe headache and blurred vision. Her brother took her to the ER, where at first they thought it was a virus, but within 24 hours, they had airlifted her to a major hospital in Chicago. A bacterial infection had attacked her heart and moved to her brain. Bleeding in the brain triggered a stroke, and she slipped into a coma. Sunday morning, Sherri's dad and mom were with her aunt as her body began to shut down to the point that her heart stopped. Even though they were able to resuscitate her, the doctors gave them little hope.

As soon as they let the family back into the room after the heart incident, Sherri's dad sent her a text and asked for prayer. Sherri was at church during a powerful time of worship when she received the message. She immediately called her dad who was sitting at the aunt's bedside. Just at that moment, I asked for those in need of healing to raise their hands and Sherri raised her hand for her aunt. Several gathered around her and laid their hands on the phone and began praying. Her dad put the phone on speaker near his sister's ear so she could hear the prayers. Then as the worship team sang "Breath of God," Sherri's dad said a reverence came into the hospital room carried by the worship from a congregation 500 miles away that changed the atmosphere. As the church worshiped and several prayed for her over the phone, she opened her eyes for the first time and squeezed Sherri's dad's hand. Thank you, Lord!

At this point, doctors did not know how badly the infection had damaged her heart and brain but she progressed dramatically over the next month. The nurses and doctors referred to her as the miracle lady. There was simply no medical reason for her to be alive. Sherri's aunt has continued to amaze people with her progress as she heals and gains mobility. The family gathered in her room that day, all testified to the change in the atmosphere while the worship played, recognizing that is when the miracle began.

FILLED WITH HIS GLORY

One of the great promises in scripture states that the earth would be filled with the glory of God (Num 14:21). This is a promise made by the Father to the Son whom He loves and as such will be fulfilled. It is inconceivable that a promise made to the Son would fail to come into full manifestation. We agree with what the prophet Isaiah foresaw as he looked into heaven and heard the refrain, *...Holy, Holy, Holy, is the LORD of hosts, The whole earth is full of His glory* (Isa 6:3). Notice that the prophet speaks in a completed tense. He sees the earth as filled even as the whole of creation waits for it to come into full manifestation. God wants us to live with this hope-filled perspective, which is as sure as the word of God.

What does that look like? When you imagine the earth filled with His glory what comes to mind? Do we see a cloud covering the earth? Do we see the light of His radiance penetrating the darkness and revealing His nature? Is it the fire of God burning the chaff and revealing the pure gold? The list could go on because the breadth of His glory proves limitless.

Glory is one of the words we use frequently, and yet sometimes we have little grasp of its real significance. We have experienced moments that we describe as glorious, and yet when asked to define it, words fail. The glory of God is beyond description as we begin to meditate on the splendor of our magnificent God.

In this chapter we are not trying to develop a theology of glory. Rather from our experience we want to broaden our understanding so that we see the glory of God at work in and through us. At the same time, we look forward with anticipation to more and more of His glory being poured out. Our focus will be the variety of ways that the glory of God manifests in this realm, literally displaying attributes of the glory of heaven here on earth.

WE SAW HIS GLORY

So what did John mean when he said, *"And the Word became flesh, and dwelt among us, and we saw His glory, glory as of the only begotten from the Father, full of grace and truth"* (John 1:14)? What did they see when they looked at Jesus? This could be a reference to the mount of transfiguration, but the majority of the commentators do not think so. They saw Him as a man but as they got to know Him, something else caught their attention. They saw glory, a glory from heaven that emanated from the Father. They saw compassion, love, power, healing, deliverance, resurrection and wisdom. Through the life of Jesus, they got a glimpse into the Father's nature. John defines the Father's nature he witnessed as *full of grace and truth.* But exactly what did the glory they saw look like? We find that the usage of the word glory in scripture falls into three broad categories.

THE GLORY OF GOD

The first way the word glory is used in scripture describes the magnificence of God and the holiness of His nature. It describes His being and the beauty, power and awe that emanates from Him. The phrase, "glory of God," and "glory of the Lord" occur numerous times in scripture. The word *glory* is used to describe honor, praise, splendor and the wonder of God. The glory of God encompasses all that He is in His nature and His attributes. The glory expresses the quality of God's character, His greatness, goodness and authority. The glory emphasizes God's moral beauty and perfection of character. We are told that Jesus has been crowned with glory. When we use the word glory in this way, it expresses the majesty that belongs to God – Father, Son and Holy Spirit.

While the word glory describes God's greatness, mystery and splendor, it also describes His standard of perfection. God's glory speaks of the absolutely perfect inward or personal excellence of Father, Son and Spirit. It is this aspect of glory that Paul refers to when he writes, *For all have sinned and fall short of the glory of God* (Rom 3:23). Sin caused us to miss the mark of His glory, a glory we have access to once again through Jesus' blood.

The Greek word for *glory doxa* means "magnificence, excellence, preeminence, dignity and grace." When we use it in relation to God, it denotes the kingly majesty that belongs to Him as the supreme Creator. It also carries a sense of the absolute perfection of the Deity. Then we add to this the Hebrew word *kabôd*, which means "weighty, and carries the idea of abundance, riches, splendor and honor." Then add to this the word *shekinah*, meaning "the dwelling," which has become the word used for God's glory by the Jews.[1] When put together, these definitions for the word glory convey a divine quality beyond our comprehension.

Heaven sings, *To Him who sits on the throne, and to the Lamb, be blessing and honor and glory and dominion forever and ever* (Rev 5:13). The song of heaven is the spontaneous declaration of all creation when they witness His majesty. The nature of God shines through in His creation, and His creation gives Him praise. His glory shapes and directs our worship – all blessing, all honor, all glory, all power. It resounds as a declaration of who He is, a testimony of thanksgiving for what He has done, which leads us to the second usage of the word glory.

GLORY AS THANKSGIVING

Frequently, the word glory is used to mean the "honor, praise and worship given to God." This includes giving testimonies of what He has done in us and through us. Paul told the church, *... that the grace which is spreading to more and more people may cause the giving of thanks to abound to the glory of God* (2 Cor 4:15). What we believe about thanksgiving matters, because it involves our receiving the grace of God, which in turn releases more of His glory. Thus giving thanks is an expression of glory, which has the power to abound – go over the top - hit critical mass. Declarations of thankfulness and praise in an assembly release the glory. This explains why the spontaneous shouts during worship release such a powerful presence.

Jesus refers to this aspect of glory after the ten lepers were healed. They all started out to show themselves to the priests but one turned back to thank Jesus for the miracle. Jesus then turned to His disciples and said, *Was no one found who turned back to give glory to God, except this foreigner"* (Luke 17:18)? Giving honor and thanksgiving to Him for what He has done is glory. This is consistent with the promise that we would overcome by both the blood of the Lamb and the word of our testimony. Learning to give Him glory in praise, thanksgiving, and by the testimony provides a key to an overcoming life. This also means that if we withhold our thanksgiving or testimony, we withhold glory that belongs to Him.

SACRIFICE OF PRAISE

God's Word teaches us to live in continual rejoicing (1 Pet 1:8), and we are told that the joy we express is full of glory. The psalmist understood this when he wrote, *The one who offers thanksgiving as his sacrifice glorifies me* (Ps 50:23). While we were writing this chapter, our worship leader lost her baby at 14 weeks. We prayed and believed with her and her husband for a miracle, but it did not come as we desired. A few days later she led worship for our Sunday service. While it would have been easy to simply go through the motions, she chose to press in, and praise erupted in the house. The more she worshiped the more it affected her team and they released glory. Praise under pressure serves as one of the purest forms of giving Him glory.

Every time we thank Him, His glory increases. Every time we give a testimony, every time we worship Him, the level of His glory rises in the earth. It is no wonder that we witness manifestations of His glory as we worship, because at its root, **worship is glory**. This leads us into the third realm of glory, His manifested presence.

MANIFESTATIONS OF GLORY

Finally, glory can describe a physical manifestation of God's presence. The word *manifestation* simply means "the invisible becoming visible." Since God is invisible, glory in this category appears as His self-manifestation. God's glory is not a substance, but rather God's presence revealed to man in visible ways. The Greek word for manifest is *phaneroo,* which means "to make visible or to make known what has been hidden or unknown." It also means "to reveal, whether by words or deeds." Thus, a manifestation of glory is simply God choosing to expose Himself to the view of those who worship Him or need Him on the earth.

Scripture lists a number of ways we can witness this display of the presence of God. As the children of Israel left Egypt they experienced the presence of God as a pillar of cloud by day and fire by night (Exod 13:21). When they complained about manna for lunch every day, God told Moses to tell them that tomorrow they would see the glory of God (Exod 16:7). The next day glory looked like the miraculous provision of quail to eat. In the tabernacle and the temple, they witnessed His glory as a cloud, which made it difficult to stand up (Lev 9:23-24, 1 Kgs 8:11).

We see the glory manifest in the New Testament when a dazzling light knocks Paul to the ground when he was confronted with Jesus (Acts 9:3). We witnessed it at the stoning of Stephen when he sees the glory of heaven. Many times in scripture the word glory is connected to healing, along with working signs, wonders and miracles.

When Jesus began His ministry, His first miracle was turning water into wine. At first glance, it doesn't appear that significant until we read John's analysis of the event. *This beginning of His signs Jesus did in Cana of Galilee, and manifested His glory, and His disciples believed in Him* (John 2:11). John looked at the miracle and said, "There it is - we just saw the glory of God." Signs and wonders serve as a manifestation of His glory. When the invisible power of God comes in a visible form, an aspect of the glory of the unseen realm has spilled over into this realm.

Through signs and wonders, we can see the unseen realm influencing the visible realm - heaven really is touching earth. When Jesus approached Lazarus' resurrection, He told Mary that if she believed, she would see the glory of God (John 11:4, 40). She thought He was referring to her future hope but He wasn't. The moment Lazarus came out of the tomb, He turned to her and said, "Didn't I say you would see the glory of God?" The miracle of raising the dead was a manifestation of glory. The world today desperately needs to witness the visible presence of His nature. They need a manifestation of His glory - the blind seeing, the deaf hearing, the lame walking, and the dead being raised.

RADIATING HIS GLORY

The writer of Hebrews tells us that Jesus ... *is the radiance of His glory and the exact representation of His nature, and upholds all things by the word of His power...* (Heb 1:3). Jesus is the radiance of the Father's glory. The word radiance here is *apaugasma,* a word used of light shining from a luminous body. The Son of God, who is one with God, is shining forth the radiance of His glory. Even in His humanity, the glory of the Father still shone through Him.

Throughout His life, Jesus manifested an *exact representation* of who God is and what He does. The Greek word *exact* here is used of "a stamp or impress."[2] The mark Jesus made on the earth conformed in every detail to the Father's nature. Jesus embodied the Father's glory – the invisible God became visible through the Son. When they looked at Jesus, they saw an exact representation of the Father's nature shining through every facet of His life and ministry.

Now it gets really interesting. In Jesus' prayer to the Father at the end of His ministry, He made a startling request. *And the glory which Thou hast given Me I have given to them; that they may be one, just as We are one* (John 17:22). The same glory that the Father gave the Son, He now releases to us. His glory at work in us produces a powerful God-like unity when, as believers, we learn to walk together. Paul tells us that the very act of accepting one another is to the glory of God (Rom 15:7). When we live together with a culture of honor, it is glorious.

But this idea of the glory of God radiating through us goes further than unity. We are called the light of the world. A primary purpose of our transformation into the image of Christ is that the world will see and know Jesus. When it refers to us as believers being transformed into His image, it does not use the same word as it does of Jesus. We are not the "exact representation." The word used here is *"reflection"* as the image in a mirror. We are to reflect His glory to the world. Moses' face shone when he encountered the glory of God, and we shine when we manifest the glory of God to the world.

We are to radiate, relate to and participate in all three aspects of the glory. We participate in the glory of God by living lives consistent with His nature and character. We allow the Holy Spirit to so work the fruit of the Spirit in us that we radiate His nature. We cry out to see more of His glory, more of His goodness, more of His nature. We want to see the glory of heaven so that we can see it manifested here on earth.

We radiate the second aspect of glory by expressing praise, adoration and worship. We release glory when we testify to the goodness of God and are thankful for all He does. We radiate His glory every time we give a testimony of His goodness. We radiate His glory when we live our lives full of gratitude for the privilege we have of partnering with heaven to see God's glory fill the earth.

We radiate the third aspect of glory by releasing the power of the kingdom into this realm. His glory radiates through us as we manifest the power of God in healing, deliverance, salvation and wholeness. With every miracle, His glory increases and His kingdom advances. The release of signs and wonders through us is a continuation of the ministry of Jesus. We read that, *... For this purpose the Son of God was manifested, that he might destroy the works of the devil* (1 John 3:8 KJV). The glory of God becomes visible for the purpose of destroying the works of the devil. This first happened with Christ, and then it happens through us as we radiate His glory. Pursue the glory of God and the enemy has no place near you.

GLORY AND GOODNESS

Manifesting His glory gives us the privilege of revealing the goodness of God. We read that God's answer to Moses' request to see His glory was to show Him all His goodness. That answer came with a revelation of God's heart of compassion. *Then the Lord passed by in front of him and proclaimed, "The Lord, the Lord God, compassionate and gracious, slow to anger, and abounding in loving-kindness and truth"* (Exod 34:6). God's goodness manifests to us and through us as grace and compassion, which flows from His nature. His grace covers our weaknesses while His compassion allows us to grow. It is a revelation of His goodness that will break us free from our history and release us into our destiny in Him.

But the goal was more than just our redemption; as His redeemed people, we are designed to radiate His glory to the world around us. We are called to demonstrate the goodness of God in such a way that the world sees Jesus and turns to Him.

When we manifest His goodness to the world, they will respond. Paul tells us that *... the kindness (goodness) of God leads you to repentance* (Rom 2:4). The judgment of God may warn people of their need to repent, but His goodness opens their hearts and calls them to repentance and salvation. It is the goodness of God that made a way for our salvation because He loved us enough to send His Son to die. The manifestation of His goodness and unconditional love leads us to repentance.

But His goodness does not stop there. His goodness gives us a new nature. His goodness removes the grave clothes and gives us a robe of righteousness. It is the goodness of God that transfers us from darkness to light, bringing us under the reign of His goodness. His goodness puts His Spirit in us, marking us as His own by legally adopting each of us as His child. With this adoption comes a new identity with all the rights and privileges of sonship. His goodness takes His own ring of authority and puts it on our finger. And His goodness heals our bodies, heals our minds, and heals our emotions.

His goodness then puts His Spirit on us so we can release His goodness to others. When we have a revelation of the goodness of God, it is impossible to hold it in; the goodness of God compels us to go out and touch others.

GLORY AND GREATER WORKS

Christ's expectation of us is that we not only do what He did, but do more. He made a promise to us, *"Truly, truly, I say to you, he who believes in Me, the works that I do shall he do also; and greater works than these shall he do; because I go to the Father"* (John 14:12). There is no limit set on the amount of kingdom blessing that can be released through us. Earlier Christ said that He had to go because if He did not, He could not send the Comforter. His return to His Father released the Holy Spirit to come and remain, shifting our focus onto following the Spirit instead of following the law.

When we know our position as sons and daughters of the King, we walk with a new confidence and authority. The Holy Spirit opens heaven to us and over us so we can hear what Jesus is declaring and then carry it out on the earth. The key here is faith in Him and in His finished work. This is not faith based on our ability to be good enough, to merit Him moving through us. It is a faith in His righteousness given to us as a gift that causes the Father to look at us in the same way that He looks at His Son.

What an awesome promise. But wait; it gets even better. In the next verse, we read that, ...*Whatever you ask in My name, that will I do, so that the Father may be glorified in the Son* (John 14:13). Every time we step out in faith, the Father gets glory from the Son's sacrifice. When we do the greater works, it is a manifestation of glory. Do notice that the promise whatever you ask is directly tied to the greater works. We would like to apply this to a new car, but in this instance the context is clear. When we step out across the chicken line, He will do amazing things. When we do the greater works, the Father is glorified in the Son.

Then the next verse gives an emphatic repetition to the promise, *If you ask Me anything in My name, I will do it* (John 14:14). A repeat for emphasis means this is a principle we must not miss. John spells out an essential and central truth that powers the greater works. When we choose to do what we were created to do, God will go to great lengths to see His glory fill the earth.

Toward the end of His ministry, Jesus expressed the true heart of radiating His glory. *I brought glory to you here on earth by completing the work you gave me to do* (John 17:4 NLT). There is nothing left undone; He fulfilled His destiny and the act of fulfilling destiny brings glory to His Father. Jesus did what He did because He knew who He was. He walked in perfect fellowship and communion with His Father. He lived under an open heaven with access to all heaven's resources, and He finished the work His Father had sent Him to do.

God created us for a purpose, which was lost in the fall but restored in Christ. Jesus now calls each of us to live by His example and fulfill our purpose. When we complete the work to which we are called, we will have brought glory to the Father.

| ENDNOTES |

CHAPTER 1

1. E. Adamson Hoebel, *Man in the Primitive World: An Introduction to Anthropology* (New York: McGraw-Hill, 1958).

2. Eric Garner, *The Art of Leadership; 500 Quotes on How to Lead Others* (Ventus Publishing April, 2009), http://bookboon.com/en/ the-art-of-leadership-ebook#reviews

CHAPTER 2

1. *Online Etymology Dictionary, s.v.* "revive," by 2016 Douglas Harper, accessed May 1, 2016, http://www.etymonline.com/index.php?al lowed_in_frame=0&search=revive.

2. *Theological Dictionary of the New Testament, abridged edition,* (Grand Rapids: W. B. Eerdmans Publishing Co., 1985).

3. Mark Batterson, *The Circle Maker* (Grand Rapids: Zondervan, 2011).

4. Lloyd M. Perry, John R. Strubhar, *Evangelistic Preaching* (Chicago: Moody Press 1979), 24.

CHAPTER 3

1. Gleason L. Archer, R. Laird Harris, *Theological Wordbook of the Old Testament* (Chicago: Moody Publishers, 2003).

2. Martin Luther, *The Epistles of St. Peter and St. Jude: Preached and Explained* (Wittemberg 1523-4), trans. by E H Gillett, (New York: Anson D. F. Randolph, 1859), 55.

3. Richard Foster, *Becoming like Christ*, Knowing and Doing C. S. Lewis Institute, Spring 2003, Accessed May 2016. http://www.cslewisinstitute. org/Becoming_Like_Christ_FullArticle

CHAPTER 4

1. *Thayer's Greek Lexicon*, Electronic Database. Copyright © 2000, 2003, 2006 by Biblesoft, Inc.

CHAPTER 5

1. *Kittle's Theological Dictionary of the New Testament* (Grand Rapids: W. B. Eerdmans, 1985), Copyright © 2000, 2003, 2006 by Biblesoft Inc.

2. The American Psychologist, Vol. 44, No. 5 (May 1989), 778.

CHAPTER 6

1. Julius Kostlin, *Life of Luther*, trans. John G. Morris (Philadelphia: Lutheran Publication Society, 1883), 440.

2. *Thayer's Greek Lexicon*, Electronic Database. Copyright © 2000, 2003, 2006 by Biblesoft, Inc.

CHAPTER 7

1. *Exegetical Dictionary of the New Testament* (Grand Rapids: W. B. Eerdmans Publishing Co., 1990).

CHAPTER 8

1. Howard Marshal, *Acts, An Introduction and Commentary*, Tyndale New Testament Commentaries (Downers Grove, IL: Inter-Varsity Press 1980), 56.

CHAPTER 9

1. Lester Sumrall, *Pioneers of Faith,* (Tulsa OK: Harrison House, 1995), 168.

2. Novatian, *A Treatise of Novatian Concerning the Trinity,* Chapter XXIX, section 251, Post-Nicene Library Vol.10, (Grand Rapids: W. B. Eerdmans Publishing Co., 1987).

CHAPTER 10

1. Reinhard Bonnke, *An Autobiography, Living a Life of Fire* (Longwood, FL: Harvester Services Inc. 2010), 242.

2. Brown, Driver & Briggs, Hebrew Lexicon, (Ontario: Woodside Bible Fellowship, 1993).

CHAPTER 11

1. John Calvin, *Calvin's Commentaries on the Bible: The Epistle of Paul to the Romans and Thessalonians,* (Grand Rapids: W. B. Eerdmans Publishing Co., 1965).

2. *Thayer's Greek Lexicon*, Electronic Database. Copyright © 2000, 2003, 2006 by Biblesoft, Inc.

3. *Theological Dictionary of the New Testament*, abridged edition, (Grand Rapids: W. B. Eerdmans Publishing Co., 1985).

4. The Pacific – Volume 58, Issues 27-52 Pp7 1908 California.

5. Leon Morris, *The First Epistle of Paul to the Corinthians,* Tyndale New Testament Commentaries, (Leicester England: Intervarsity Press, 1989), 193.

6. *Thayer's Greek Lexicon*, Electronic Database. Copyright © 2000, 2003, 2006 by Biblesoft, Inc.

CHAPTER 12

1. *The Jewish Encyclopedia, s.v.* "shekinah", by Kaufmann Kohler, 1906, accessed May 15, 2016. http://www.jewishencyclopedia.com/search?utf8=%E2%9C%93&keywords=shekinah&commit=search

2. James Strong, *New Exhaustive Strong's Numbers and Concordance with Expanded Greek-Hebrew Dictionary,* (Nashville:Thomas Nelson, 2010).